# 12 Wicker Baskets

Collected
Fragments
from

# The Mystery of Presence

## PHILIP KRILL

**author**HOUSE®

*AuthorHouse™*
*1663 Liberty Drive*
*Bloomington, IN 47403*
*www.authorhouse.com*
*Phone: 833-262-8899*

*Published by AuthorHouse  09/10/2021*

*ISBN: 978-1-6655-3734-6 (sc)*
*ISBN: 978-1-6655-3735-3 (e)*

*Print information available on the last page.*

*Editing Assistance:  Carrie Lee Hershberger, Jessica Livengood*

To

Mary Catherine Williams

She who lives 'in Spirit'

"So they gathered them up and filled twelve baskets with fragments from the five barley loaves, left by those who had eaten."

*John 6:13*

# Contents

# Introduction

After Jesus of Nazareth fed the five thousand with five loaves and two fishes (Lk. 9:10-17), his apostles collected twelve wicker baskets of leftover fragments. The perfection of these numbers - seven and twelve - indicates the Divine Abundance of everything that comes from the hands of God.

Mystics of the ancient Orient also knew of Divine Abundance. They called this Mystery *Saccidananda,* a Hindu term that connotes the divine Bliss (*Ananda*) that arises within us when our Awareness (*Chit*) rests in Being (*Sat*), not in thinking. The experience of *Saccidananda* is what Jesus meant when he said, '*The kingdom of God is within you*' (Lk. 17:28).

One way of entering the kingdom of God, or experiencing *Saccidananda,* is to contemplate the *Mystery of Presence. Presence,* like the Mystery of God, is impossible to describe, yet, is as undeniable as it is indefinable. *Presence* is the experience of being completely Open: alert, attentive, receptive, yet altogether empty of thought and devoid of agenda. Presence is the experience of transcendental Awareness that intuits the infinity of Being, and imparts such Divine Bliss that we sense it can only be coming from God.

This book is a collection of fragments gleaned from the experience of *Presence.* They are purposely random and repetitive, bespeaking the ever-new, ever-greater nature of the Mystery of *Presence.* They are given here to help the reader be present, and grow in contemplative prayer.

*August 15, 2021*
*Feast of the Assumption of the Blessed Virgin Mary*

# 1st

## Wicker Basket

*Philip Krill*

Consciousness is the Presence of God within us. Our capacity for Awareness - or Presence - is a participation in God's own Spirit.

God's Spirit makes possible our self-transcendence. In self-transcendence, we experience the Peace that *'passes all understanding'* (cf. Phil. 4:7). This is the Peace of God, which is also our own essential nature and destiny.

The *situation* we are in never really matters. The moment we place our situation in the Space of Awareness, we transcend it. It has no power to harm us.

Pain is inevitable, but suffering is optional. Suffering comes from thinking evil thoughts or projecting negative labels upon any situation.

In the Space of accepting Awareness, we are delivered from suffering. In the Space of resistance, we are lost to it. Salvation and suffering are equally available in any situation.

Everything we resist in life grows stronger in its power over us. Letting go (*Gelassenheit*) is the key to being delivered from suffering.[1]

---

[1] See my book, *Gelassenheit: Day-by-Day with Meister Eckhart.*

To let go is not to become lazy or stupid. It is to create enough Space in any situation that the Wisdom of God can appear. Presence is the passage from hell into the Kingdom of God.

Every problem is an opportunity to practice deeper Presence. Simply being present to any problem, we begin to dissolve it. Simple Awareness is the antidote to what, emotionally, is ailing us at any given moment.

God's first recorded words are, *'Let there be light'* (cf. Gen. 1:3). Translation: 'Let there be Consciousness, let there be Awareness, let there be *'Letting-go-ness' (Gelassenheit)*. 'Letting be' is a synonym for the Will and Presence of God.

Whenever we say, 'Let it be' to any person, place, thought, emotion, or situation, the Presence of God arises within us. 'Letting be' is the Space in which the Presence and the Peace of God manifests themselves.

Mary became the Mother of God when she said, *'Let it be to me according to your word'* (cf. Lk. 1:38). The Power of God arises within us when we *consent* to the form of the present moment.

Time is relative to our state of Acceptance or Awareness. Time drags on when our minds are full of negative thoughts. By contrast, time flies when we are having fun. In the Space of *No-thought*, time disappears.

Pure, unadulterated, attentive Presence is the definition of Love. Presence - Love - has no agenda other than Allowing the other to be just as they are.

Presence is the Space of attentive, open Receptivity in which the 'other' feels welcome without condition. This Space is sometimes called the Kingdom of God.

Guilt about the past and fear of the future are twin departures from Presence and from Peace. They are futile exercises in egoic insanity. *'Nothing that is real can be threatened, nothing unreal exists. Therein lies the Peace of God.'*[2]

Resistance to what is at the present moment takes us out of heaven and plunges us into hell. The moment we become Aware of our terrible plight, however, we are delivered from it. The trick is to extend this period of Awareness, prolonging our respite in Presence.

It is never not Now. It is always only Now. *The Power of Now* communicates the Presence of God.[3]

---

[2] *Course in Miracles.*

[3] See Eckhart Tolle, *The Power of Now.*

Creation *ex nihilo* - 'out of nothing' - happens all the time. Death and resurrection are the warp and woof of the cosmos. Every act of 'Letting go' (*Gelassenheit*) results in an immediate 'lifting up'. Every act of Surrender brings satisfaction. Every act of Dispossession (*Kenosis*) brings a Peace that surpasses understanding. Nothing is ever lost through dying that something greater is not immediately brought to life.

The power of 'Allowing' is unlimited. If we think of ourselves as a 'spacious Presence of Allowing,' all who enter our orbit will feel its healing power.

The phrase, 'We are only human,' is often used to justify egoic insanity. To be truly human is to be delivered from ego by being spiritually present. Practicing Presence is the essence of spirituality.

'Being present' means cultivating a spacious Awareness. In the Emptiness of Presence, ideas and emotions arise and dissolve without affecting our deepest selves.

Suffering comes from mentally resisting the shape of the present moment. Those who suffer tend to *identify* themselves with their suffering. Until they learn to disidentify with their stories of woe, they remain asleep in their personal nightmares.

Be the Space in which others can be themselves. Be the Presence in which all who come to you find welcoming Acceptance. Be the person without agenda in whose company all feel well-received and understood. Therein lies the truth of real holiness.

*Kenosis = theosis. Self-emptying (Kenosis, Gelassenheit)* is the path to self-realization. Dying to self is the means to self-discovery.

Enlightenment doesn't do away with the self. It reveals the self as *participating in* a Higher Self that we may call 'God'.

The ego and the self are not identical. We must lose our ego to find our true self. This occurs in the experience of self-transcendence.

Self-transcendence is the image of God within us. It also communicates the Presence of God to us. Those who are still suffering are not yet aware of their self-transcendence. They are not conscious of the Higher Self, silently calling them to awaken from their spiritual coma.

God uses whatever it takes to awaken us from egoic unconsciousness. Often God uses suffering to deliver us from suffering. Some enter Presence only when they become sick and tired of being sick and tired. In such a moment of self-awareness, a new life, a new world opens up before them. Some call this Awakening 'eternal life' or 'the kingdom of God'. Others call it 'getting sober' or 'recovering from addiction'. As they say in Alcoholics Anonymous: 'It's not the drinkin' that makes you stinkin' but the stinkin' thinkin' that gets you drinkin.'"

Children are taught to be present when they are put in 'time out'. There, they are invited to experience self-transcendence, i.e., to reflect on their behavior, and so to 'come to their senses.' If the adults who put children in 'time out' practiced it more often themselves, they may find that fewer of their children would need it.

There is no end to the second-chances available to us to awaken from egoic death. Every failure is an opportunity to enter the life of Peace, joy, and serenity that comes through enlightened Letting-go. (*Gelassenheit*).

Enlightenment, salvation, is always close at hand. It happens the moment we *accept* any situation we are tempted to find unacceptable. Recognizing our resistance to reality, we release it. This Space of *Releasement (Gelassenheit)* is an in-breaking of the kingdom of God.

The great thing about Acceptance - and hence, of salvation - is that nothing can defeat it and we can embrace it everywhere. If we find something unacceptable, we can always *accept our refusal to accept*. When we do this we are saved from the shame and guilt that result from resistance.

Certain phrases in our vernacular encourage the practice of Presence: *'Take a time out,' 'Take a step back,' 'Take a deep breath.'* Enlightenment comes from living in the Space of the Step Back, the Deep Breath, the Time Out.

Enlightenment, Awakening, Salvation, 'Going to heaven,' 'Eternal life': all these terms refer to the same thing - the Mystery of Presence, i.e., learning how to 'be present' with every person we meet and in every situation we encounter.

The *Power of the Now* is also the Power of the *Tao*.

The experience of Presence is never-old, always New. It cannot be grasped once and for all. It requires a moment-by-moment Alertness to the freshness of the Now.

Presence is alert Attentiveness, spacious Awareness. It requires willingness, Openness, and Receptivity. Any form of mental resistance prevents Presence from making itself felt.

Presence is another word for '*God.*' Indefinable and incapable of being objectified, Presence is more real than anything else in our lives. Presence is the Unconditioned Mystery that makes our sentient experience possible.

*Non-identification with our thoughts* is the quickest way into Presence. Mind is an *epiphenomenal* manifestation of Presence. Presence makes thinking possible, thinking does not define Presence.

The fact that we can be Aware of our own thinking processes demonstrates the transcendental nature of Presence. *Awareness of our thinking* is not another form of thinking. It is a pre-conceptual Apprehension in which our concepts appear and disappear.

We call those 'saints' who live in a state of continuous Presence. Saints perceive the world as a *kaleidoscope* of appearing and disappearing beauty, a world of ever-changing forms, communicating the infinite Presence of the Formless.

Saints see no evil, hear no evil, speak no evil. They are not imprisoned or discouraged by their thoughts. Because they live in the Space of No-mind (*Mushin*), they see reality more clearly, and more perfectly, than anyone else.

Problems are unknown in the Space of Presence. In Presence, problems reveal themselves as figments of our imaginations. They are nothing but thought forms imposed upon reality. They blind us to the truth about reality and inhibit us from dealing wisely with the world.

Problems are a product of ruminating about the past or the future. We regret the past and fear the future. But perfect Presence casts out all fear and dissolves all guilt. Guilt and shame are hallmarks of the ego, and the ego is identification with the thoughts of the mind.

Suffering sometimes activates Presence. Suffering serves us like a warning light on the dashboard. If we have the Presence of mind to pull over, we can spare ourselves a mental meltdown. To acknowledge suffering is to transcend it.

Presence is making contact with an Intelligence - a Wisdom - that transcends thought. Presence always brings a feeling of Aliveness, freshness and promise. Thinking brings a sense of heaviness, density and pressure. *Continuous joy* is the experience of those who practice Presence.

Anything we think or say about ourselves beyond '*we are*' is a lie. It is an egoic identification with an idea. It has no basis in truth.

Presence is something greater than forgiveness. Forgiveness is Presence experienced through the lens of ego. Only egoic insanity needs forgiveness. For those who live in Presence, forgiveness is beside the point.

Pure Listening is another synonym for Presence. In moments of pure Listening, one is without agenda, and therefore without ego. Presence becomes palpable wherever true Listening takes place. *Sat* (being), *chit* (mind), *ananda* (Bliss) - *Saccidanānda* - connotes the divine Bliss that arises within us when our minds rest in Being, not in thinking.

We are in a state of Presence when we know ourselves as fields of alert, spacious Awareness. We fall into ego when thinking occludes simple Attentiveness. The egoic mind is infinitely voracious and never satisfied. It destroys Presence whenever we let it.

Presence is never defeated by any action of the ego. The ego, in fact, is its own worst enemy. For when we become aware of the ego, we have already risen above it. The trick to *Saccidanānda* is learning how to extend this period of Recognition.

Presence is a state of unwavering Recognition, a place of unflinching Awareness. It is the practice of unconditional Acceptance. Presence is the Space in which we *allow* all objects to arise and dissolve, without judgment, without anxiety, without interpretation. The Consciousness that we are is the Space in which reality is permitted to be. Bliss arises whenever we practice this kind of trans-mental Presence.

'Noticing' is another portal into Presence. When we simply *notice* something - allowing the form of the present moment to show itself as it is - we are in a state of Presence. We need be no more negatively affected by what we notice than a movie screen is impacted by the images projected upon it.

Practicing Presence does not make us indifferent to what is happening in the world. It simply keeps us from identifying with the objects of our perception.

Presence gives us the interior freedom to discern any situation wisely. Wisdom arises in the Space of Presence. Everything else is an illusion of the egoic intellect.

Every disturbance of Presence is an opportunity for us to recognize it as such and return to Presence. It is the power of Presence that recognizes when it has been disturbed, and, in that very recognition and Acceptance, returns us to itself.

Presence, recognition and Acceptance are identical: as noticing, allowing, permitting, receiving, embracing, welcoming, and surrendering. These are all interchangeable terms for the Mystery of 'Letting be' (*Gelassenheit*). We also call this 'being present'.

The power of Presence is infinite. The power of letting-be is infinite. No matter what the disturbances - no matter what problems the ego manufactures - the moment we let them be, the power of Presence has triumphed over them.

No matter how many times the ego interrupts our practice of Presence, the practice of Acceptance always overcomes it. Eventually the ego tires of kicking against the goad. Ego detests being recognized for what it is, but, once recognized, is dissolved. Ultimately ego gives way to the infinite power of Presence.

# 2nd

## Wicker Basket

Presence is infinite because it accepts every disturbance of the ego and grows stronger as a result. In the end, egoic suffering becomes its own cure. Alert to a disturbance in its Force, the power of Presence befriends the attacks of the ego and miraculously turns its enemy into its ally.

Presence is the alchemical power of Acceptance within us that takes the leaden thoughts of the ego and immediately turns them to gold.

Practicing Presence is learning how to become a 'Space of Allowing'. In this 'Space of Allowing,' we let go of our mind-streams related to the world of form. We abide blissfully in the place of No mind, a place that is alert, attentive, yet empty of thoughts and open to the infinite Horizon of Being.

Once we become aware of our problems, we are on the way to overcoming them. In Presence, awareness quickly expands to Acceptance, and Acceptance brings relief. The key is not falling asleep again and re-entering the nightmare of our thoughts.

Presence becomes possible when we see that we have a *transcendental* relationship with ourselves. We have an *internal observer*, i.e., an internal witness who can watch, without interpretation, all that we are doing. Both 'we's' are us, but our deepest identity is found in our internal witness.

Our capacity for self-transcendence does not end by noticing that we have an internal observer. For we can observe this internal observer, and we can witness this internal witness. This process can continue *ad infinitum*.

Because our nature is truly transcendental, there is no limit to the depths to which we can know ourselves, and no limits to the degree that we can know the One ('God') who makes this self-transcendence possible.

When we accept our non-Acceptance of any situation, we have risen above our resistance and entered the Peace of Presence.

Everything that interrupts the practice of being present is an opportunity to deepen our experience of Presence by noticing the interruption and just letting it be. The conscious Acceptance of the interruption is always a deepening, not a dissolution, of Presence.

Presence is the Space of Allowing that accepts all, touches all, and heals all.

Presence never fails to dissolve the insanity that enters it. Like an out-of-control child in the loving arms of a care-giver, histrionics eventually peter out in the welcoming embrace of someone who knows how to be present. All problems, difficulties in life, and suffering are but so many invitations from Presence to return to Presence. It is the power of Presence within us that allows us to 'catch ourselves' anytime we have drifted away from being present. The practice of Mindfulness is identical with the practice of Presence. Neither description involves the word *'God,'* but in mindfulness and practicing Presence are where the Presence of God is found.

To be a true believer in 'God' we must become a *practical atheist.* We must recognize that our concepts and images of God are produced by the mind (ego).

Presence is the experience of God loving God's-self in us.

In the state of Presence, nothing is experienced as a means to an end. Because Presence is a Space of unconditional letting-go, objects that appear in Presence have a density of their own and are received as ends in themselves. A chair, for example, is not 'a chair,' but that which some people label as such. The uniqueness of any object, when experienced in Presence, is not known by categorization.

Presence sanctifies everything and everyone. It creates a Space for the other to be itself in a way that can only be described as sacred.

Presence alone teaches, heals. Only words that come from Presence impact their hearers in a positive way. Only actions that come from Presence have the power to make their recipients whole.

Presence is perhaps the best cypher we could choose for '*God*'. Presence is always *self*-Presence, and 'God' is the Power that makes self-Presence possible. This may be why God describes God's-self as 'I AM who am' (Ex. 3:14). Translation: 'I am THAT from which anything is. I AM the Power that allows all that is to be present. I AM the Presence that affords you a share in the power of Presence.'

Problems untangle themselves in the Space of Presence. When we let go of results, results produce themselves. When we let the bird fly free, the bird returns to us.

Presence is another - perhaps better word - for Love. When we love someone we know how to give that person our undivided Attention. We know how to be totally present. In the Space of Presence, persons know themselves to be loved.

Presence always brings Peace. In the Space of radical Attentiveness, ego disappears and serenity arises. The power of the Now is palpable.

Presence purifies all that is placed within it. Practicing Presence is, as it were, a spiritual desalinization process. That which enters into it always comes out pure, clear and refreshing.

Presence serves as an antidote to the poison of personalization. When we take things personally, we die spiritually. We transcend personalization when we practice Presence. In the experience of Presence, our personal problems dissolve and even egoic insults from others lose their power to harm us.

In the Space of Presence, a certain relaxation happens naturally. Our eyes soften, our grip loosens, and a Peace that passes mental understanding arises within us. 'Going to heaven' means remaining as long as possible in this state of complete surrender to the form of the present moment.

Be-like-water: non-resistant, completely receptive, invisible, unassuming, life-giving, conforming completely to objects placed in it, yet more powerful than any other substance, dissolving even rock to create grand canyons. Relaxing into Presence means becoming like water. Ultimately, Presence is not something we only practice, it is something we essentially *are*. When we are present to others, we *are* the Presence they encounter, we *are* the Space of the unqualified Acceptance they experience. Be the Space, be the Presence.

In Presence we are still ourselves, not as ego but as spirit. We are who we are. Not only is this true of the One we call 'God' (cf. Ex. 3:14) but also of each of us. *Individual identity is not dissolved in Presence*, only egoic identity with its adjectival labels. We are not indistinguishable drops of Awareness destined for dissolution in the Ocean of Consciousness, but neither are we self-sustaining individuals who practice Presence on our own. Our lives are hidden with God in the Mystery of Presence.

Power in teaching or preaching comes from abiding in Presence. When we have to think about what we are saying, the power of Presence is diminished. Only words spoken from a place of Presence have the power to impact the listener. This is especially true of words about Presence.

The best thoughts come from a place *beyond thought*, i.e., from Presence. In the No-mind Space of alert Attentiveness, creative thinking occurs. Creativity is a function of abiding in Presence, not of mental activity.

Geniuses are generally aware that their brilliance comes through them, not from them. Often they cannot tell you how they know what they know, or how they do what they do. They just do it. (The *just* in the previous sentence hints at the power of Presence.)

There is no bottom to the abyss of self-surrender indicated by the phrase, 'practicing Presence'.

Method is the saving grace for those not yet steeped in Presence. Virtuoso violinists or pianists don't methodically finger their violins. Great artists do not paint by numbers. 'Outside-the-box' does not begin to convey how other-worldly is the inspiration given to creative geniuses. If they are self-aware, they are humbled by it.

In Presence, nothing is pressured, nothing is compelled. Presence is a Space of empty Attentiveness. Rules and regulations are foreign and irrelevant to those who practice Presence. In the Space of Presence, everything happens naturally, organically. Nothing is forced. Perfect freedom pervades the place of Presence.

Reincarnation describes the fate of those who are caught in endless cycles of egoic re-definition. They are continually being reborn into new iterations of egoic identity. Seeking repeated identification with some external identity, they remain unaware of their essential identity as personal Presence. The ever-changing descriptions they give themselves function like layers of bad cosmetics. Far from bringing them beauty, they obscure their inherent perfection. Cultivating Presence is the end of egoic reincarnation.

Reactivity is a sure sign of ego. *Awareness* of these egoic eruptions is the conquest of the ego through the arising Presence.

We lose our egoic identity when we experience ourselves as fields of self-conscious Presence. Self-consciousness is not the same thing as self-assertion. Self-*consciousness* is sensing our own Presence in the Presence of a power greater than ourselves. We do not lose our identity in the Mystery of Presence. But it eludes our description and is hidden from us in God.

The Mystery of 'us' is not an illusion. The power of Presence does not obliterate personal identity. Presence is a Power that simultaneously envelops and establishes us as an *'image and likeness'* of Itself (cf. Gen. 1:26).

We are one with, yet distinct from, the Mystery of Presence. Presence *flows through us*, perfecting, rather than annihilating, our unique identities in Presence. We become theophanic with Presence when we put no acts of ego in its way.

Joy is the most visible earmark of living in Presence.

Every challenge in life is an invitation to enter more deeply into Presence. Letting go, standing back, taking a deep breath: these are the simple ways of putting *Space* around life's challenges and neutralizing their power to disturb us.

Mistakes - sins - are unknown in Presence. Becoming aware of our mistakes is their instant redemption. Our mistakes disappear as soon as we identify with our Higher Self who acknowledges them. For that Higher Self - our true self - such mistakes do not exist.

From the standpoint of Presence, sin is an illusion. Guilt, shame, condemnation, etc. are concoctions of the ego. They are forms of temporary insanity, departures from 'being present'. In *awareness* of sin, there is no sin. Once we realize that Awareness - Presence - is our true self (or identity in God), our capacity for sin evaporates (cf. 1 Jn. 3:9).

The human mind is insatiable in its desire to create reality by defining it. Ego invents concepts and labels *ad infinitum* to control what it perceives. In so doing it is oblivious to the deeper possibility of 'letting go' (*Gelassenheit*). Presence makes true discernment possible.

Wisdom comes from abiding in Presence. Worry and anxiety come from listening to the voices in our head. The mind creates problems. Practicing Presence brings the Peace *'that passes all understanding'* (cf. Phil. 4:7).

Presence is every person's true nature. Everything else is an insane identification with the illusions of the egoic mind.

Egoic thinking is always heavy, constricting, full of itself. Those who live beyond mind in Presence, however, not only see the truth of things more clearly, they also experience continuous wonder, joy, delight and Peace. They watch in awe as the kaleidoscopic world of objects arises and dissolves before them.

The ego cannot survive the power of the present moment. Ego draws its life from ruminating on the past and the future. Ego does not know how to be present to itself. It is tone-deaf to self-transcendence. Transcending ego by being present is the essence of salvation.

Practicing Presence is the escape from the hell created by the ego.

Our capacity for Presence is the life of 'God' within us. It is also a Mystery greater than us. Whenever we make the effort simply to 'become aware' of who we are and what is happening around us, we are one step closer to what some call 'the kingdom of God'.

We are none of the things we think we are, nor are we in any way defined by what we do or don't do. 'Who we are' eludes classification. It is the ego that seeks to classify. It is the Power of Presence that renders all classification impossible.

A person who is present communicates the power of Presence to others. Even external circumstances are positively impacted by a person who is completely and serenely present.

Persons upset by the action of the ego have a difficult time with persons in Presence. The collision between ego and Presence is palpable. Confronted with Presence, the ego either runs away or dissolves.

Presence in one person awakens Presence in another.

Histrionics and dramatics disappear in the place of Presence. Silence pushes any crisis to its point of dissolution.

Being present means experiencing ourselves as personal mysteries of thoughtless awareness. In Presence, we have a healing effect upon those we encounter.

Spirituality means doing all we can to remain in a constant state of Presence. This is not something, strictly speaking, that we can 'do'. It is a state of being that we can recognize and cultivate. Presence is our very nature at our most foundational depths. The most we can to is *consent* to being in action what we are in essence: Presence.

When Jesus said to Mary Magdalene, *'Do not cling to me'* (Jn. 20:17), he was telling her that Presence is not something that can be grasped or held on to, but only a Mystery that can be experienced. Presence resists all objectification. It transcends the world of objects and actions, yet it is the elusive condition that makes wise thinking and acting possible.

Presence functions in the world of perceptions like negative Space functions in every great work of art. It is the indefinable background that makes our perception of the foreground possible.

# 3rd

# Wicker Basket

No matter how hard one tries to identify negative Space in a work of art, it always recedes from view. So too with 'being present': The mysterious Space of Presence is always one step ahead of - or removed from - our focal attention.

*Listening* tends to communicate the power of Presence. Pure Listening is pure Presence. It is a Space of No-mind in which all things are welcomed; yet, it is never over-crowded.

Listening is the way of *unknowing*. It is a state of unprejudiced Openness. It knows nothing other than being available to the other. In this state of intentional Emptiness, intimacy and revelation can occur.

Speaking - as opposed to Listening - is fraught with danger. Often it is nothing other than verbal mind-streams colliding with each other. A whirlpool of egoic drama is created by persons who speak more than they listen.

Thinking proliferates like wildfire. *Gaps in thinking* where Presence could arise are closed off. Spaciousness is lost in a cascade of words and ideas. Judgments and interpretations eliminate our capacity to be present. Presence suffocates in a maelstrom of mental activity.

The world of the ego is a delusional system made mad by guilt and shame. In Presence, by contrast, guilt and shame cannot exist. When we are totally present, ego is suspended. It momentarily disappears. Ego re-appears the instant we enter back into our mind-streams.

Entering the peaceful Space of Presence is possible in every life situation, even those we label as tragic or unbearable. Near death experiences confirm that death itself is a prime opportunity to experience pure Presence.

Perfect Presence drives out all fear, even the fear of death (cf. 1 Jn. 4:18).

Drama is the opposite of Presence. Recognizing the drama for what it is disarms the drama. Huffing and puffing find no place in Presence. Presence always takes the wind out the ego's sails.

Ego creates anxiety by trying to make the story of our lives work. But we are not the stories we tell ourselves. We are the ones who can *see* that such stories are fairy tales of the ego - illusory and ultimately insane.

Looking for purpose in our stories about the past or the future is futile. Our primary purpose in life is to be altogether present to the present moment. Future life is an illusion of the ego. Even if there were a future, it would be experienced as something happening Now.

We will never be closer to God than we are Now because it is never not Now.

Non-resistance to the present moment is the portal to Peace. In the Space of Acceptance, serenity arises.

Ego feeds on abstract concepts. Presence fasts from such mental indulgence. Spiritual people do not mistake spiritual *ideas* for the *experience of Presence*. They know that if they are *thinking* about God, the immediacy of God is eluding them.

Presence is attentive awareness, virginal Openness, unimpeded Receptivity, spacious allowance, total surrender, unconditional Acceptance, perfect Letting go, absolute Letting be (*Gelassenheit*). It is not, however, without understanding. In the Space of Presence, *Wisdom* arises.

Stillness speaks when we let Being be. Love and understanding appear in our acts of complete Acceptance.

The *'fall from grace'* is the forgetfulness of Being. As soon as we lose a sense of the present moment, we find ourselves cast out from the Paradise of Presence. We will languish there as long as it takes for us to *'come to our senses'* and return to the redemptive power of Presence (cf. Lk. 15:17). Practicing Presence is to know God beyond 'God,' Self beyond self. It is a raid on the Unspeakable.

Awareness of Awareness is our essential identity, yet it is not devoid of personal uniqueness. To be unique is not necessarily to be egoistic. The one who is aware that she is Aware is nevertheless an irreducible *she*. Personal identity, even in Presence, never dissolves into a pantheistic soup of Consciousness.

The real 'us' is 'behind' all the thoughts in our heads. We are most truly those *capable of thinking*, not primarily those who engage in actual thinking. The depths of ourselves, experienced as *transcendence*, cannot be reduced to thinking, much less to our brain activity.

We are never that with which we identify. We are always greater than that which we name ourselves. Our 'we-are-ness' always precedes the fact that we are this or that. Before we are this or that, we *are*. It is this 'we-are-ness' that constitutes our essential identity in God. We are they who are *in* the One who is I AM (cf. Ex. 3:14-15).

The Mystery of Presence is the experience of being present to ourselves, enveloped and sustained by a Power *greater than* ourselves. Persons who are present experience themselves as in a non-completive co-inherence with an infinite Presence that makes their personal Presence possible.

God is the Mystery of Presence of which our ability to experience Presence partakes. The Presence we call 'God' precedes and makes possible our transcendental Awareness.

Who we *think* we are is never who we really *are*. We are the one who *knows* that we are not what we think we are. But those 'who know that they are not what they think they are' can never be known. They can only know *that* they know. *Who* they are always escapes direct knowing.

Forgetfulness of Presence is the Source of all fear, doubt and insecurity. It makes possible the arising of the ego. Our Awareness of the ego, however, immediately tempers its power. Presence is the death of the ego and the birth of the spirit.

Every appearance of the ego, as it triggers Awareness, is its own nemesis. Ego is inherently self-destructive. The very racket it causes, because it awakens Presence, makes the ego its own worst enemy.

Ego is personal identification with the *labels* of our mind-streams. *Dis-identification* with personal description is the first step to personal discovery.

Presence arises when the present moment has absolute priority for us. In being present to the present moment, ego disappears, but *we* do not. We are those who *are* before we do this or that, including practicing Presence.

Everyone experiences pain but suffering is always optional. Suffering comes from telling ourselves dreadful stories about the pain we are experiencing. Eliminate the story, and the suffering dissolves.

Awareness is the unfailing solvent for egoic activity. To become Aware is to find Space. To find Space is to find Relief. Once the relief of 'stepping back' becomes greater than the pain of plunging in, we stop plunging in.

Paradise is sustaining a state of continuous Presence. This implies neither inactivity nor stoic indifference. It means living a life of continual Mindfulness.

The fires of hell singe our souls when we depart from Presence. Guilt, shame and remorse from the past, fear, doubt and insecurity about the future: these are the hot coals that stoke the fires of hell.

The Space of Presence is the Space of *No-thought* ((*Mushin*). *No-thought* does not mean no Awareness. On the contrary, it means such acute, arrested Awareness that thought itself is temporarily suspended. It is the Space of immediate, undivided, but thought-less Attention. It is a beautiful thing to behold, especially when we are recipients of it.

Being present means entering into a state of relaxed Receptivity, of alert Attentiveness, of childlike Wonderment. It is a Space of Beholding, devoid of anything but pure Appreciation.

Appreciation precedes analysis. Awareness precedes explanation. Interpretation obscures the unadulterated beauty of Beholding.

Appreciation, Awareness, Attentiveness are beyond thinking. They are synonyms for Presence.

Being present is always prior to, and more powerful than, being right or wrong. Debate, discussion, disagreement and violence are what we get when we step out of Presence.

Presence is intoxicating because it is of the Spirit. Thinking feels like a bad hangover after we have experienced the inebriation of Presence.

When we *look at* our impatience, we do so from a place *beyond* impatience. When we *notice* we are getting angry, we do so from a place that is *not* upset. When we *listen* to our jealousy speaking, we do so from a *non-jealous* standpoint. Where is that standpoint? Where is that place? It is both our essential nature and a Mystery greater than ourselves. It is the place of Presence where we are present to ourselves and also Aware of our own Awareness.

Looking, noticing, Listening: these are portals to Presence and openings into God. They are inherently transcendent, and therefore Infinite. We can *look at our looking*; we can *notice our Noticing*; we can *listen to our Listening*. This can go on *ad infinitum*. And since we *are* these things, we also partake of Infinity.

Are Presence and God identical? Not exactly. God is glimpsed in the experience of Presence, but always as the unthematic *Horizon* in which even the experience of Presence takes place. God is the indefinable *Background* to every possible foreground. God is the world's *Negative Space*.

The deeper we enter into our internal observer - ourselves beyond ego - the more we come home to ourselves. The more present to ourselves we become, the more settled we become. Presence is Acceptance and Acceptance is Peace.

We are never the ones we *think* we are. We are always only those who are able to *observe* they think they are something other than 'they are'.

As our *internal Witness* grows stronger than our mind-identified lower self (ego), we begin to awaken. We are fully awake - enlightened - when our internal observer no longer has ears for the voices in our heads.

The Power of Presence in us always speaks to the Power of Presence in the other. *Cor ad cor loquitur:* heart speaks to heart.[4] This communication is beyond mind, beyond thought. Yet it is more real than any other communication.

---

[4] The motto of St. John Henry Cardinal Newman.

No human being needs fixing. Our capacity for Presence is the defining essence of being human. To be alive is to be Aware. To be knowingly Aware is to be fully alive, fully human.

Histrionics are the stuff of the ego. At the same time, they are opportunities to return to a state of Presence. Acquiring an ear for drama, the Awakened person returns to Presence. In Presence, histrionics and drama completely dissolve.

Become conscious of the Mystery of Awareness that you are. Rest in that place. It is the antechamber to the Kingdom of God.

Being there as 'Spacious Awareness' is the same as saying, 'We are'. *'Being-there-ness'* is the definition of being present. 'We are' = 'We are there for you.' It is only the ego that blinds us to our inherent nature as *'being-there-for-ness.'*

Beauty is the Power of Presence manifesting Itself in the world of form. True beauty always arrests us. It puts a momentary stop to our thoughts and opens us powerfully to Presence. Remaining in the Space of arrested No-thought is the way, not only to appreciate beauty, but to become beautiful. Presence beatifies.

Presence is empty of thought but saturated with Power. It is the Power of the same Nothingness from which the Big Bang proceeded.

Presence is the absolute Relinquishment of the mind as a means of control. It is an intentional Evacuation of thought as an instrument of possessiveness. This mental vacuum - this Nothingness - partakes of the creative power of God. It is a mystical Fulness (*Pleroma*) in which all creative genius appears.

In the Space of No-agenda - *Presence* - the most perfect Intuitions and answers appear. Presence is the thought-less Attentiveness in which the most unimaginably beautiful inspirations arise.

To retain a sense of Presence, we must come back again and again to the realization that those who *see* their anxiety are not themselves anxious; those who *become aware* of their unsettledness are not themselves unsettled; those who *notice* their mendacity are not themselves mendacious.

# 4th

# Wicker Basket

The Space of Noticing is the Space of Presence. It is the place of No-mind, yet it is also the place of super-essential Alertness, Attentiveness, Receptivity. It is, in fact, the dwelling place of God.

The place of No-mind is not the place of *no self*. It is the place where the *true self* is present but *hidden* from itself. The philosophy of *Advaita* is not quite true.[5] Loss of ego is not loss of self. It is only the loss of the *false* self (ego). Knowing ourselves as Awareness does not eliminate a unique identity called 'us'. Identity and ego are never simply identical, otherwise there would be no 'we' to notice or say such things.

Every Pause in the mind-stream is an in-breaking of the Kingdom of God. Such Pauses are oases in the desert of continuous thought. The goal of life is to depart the desert of thinking and abide continually in the oasis of Presence.

Time and thinking are co-extensive. One implies the other, yet neither is ultimately real. Our level of Presence determines the reality of time for us.

Whenever there is a gap in thinking, the possibility for Awakening arises. When our mental guard is down the face of God can appear. Taking a step back, taking a deep breath, taking a time out: these are simple ways of entering Presence.

---

[5] *Advaita* is the philosophy of physical and metaphysical non-duality.

The ego flourishes in time but the spirit in Presence. When we are fully present to someone or something, time disappears. Hand-wringing and ulcers evaporate when Presence replaces thinking as our default position.

Direct experience happens only in the present moment. Nothing real exists in the past or the future. Even if we have a memory of the past, such memories always occur only in the present. When the future arrives - if there were such a thing - it can only appear as another Now. We search in vain for past or future. These are nothing but mental abstractions, and even they come to us only in the present moment.

Acceptance overcomes everything that comes our way. All resistance eventually dissolves in the ocean of Acceptance. Non-resistance conquers the greatest evils.

That which we struggle against grows in its power over us. Rivalry is an exercise in mutual monster-making. Soft eyes dissolve the mendacious grimace. Kind answers turn away wrath (cf. Prv. 29:8).

Learning how to be fully present to the present moment is the spiritual equivalent of splitting the atom. The release of creative energy is unimaginable.

The Presence of 'God' is experienced in alert Attentiveness to the power of the present moment. The act of 'being present' reveals a Presence that makes 'being present' possible. This indefinable Presence is what is hinted at when we use the word 'God'.

Presence is God loving God's-self in and through the self-aware person.

Thinking cannot solve the problems thinking creates.

Wisdom comes from a sustained 'intuition of Being.' It comes from retaining a felt-sense of our own *we-are-ness*. The activity of the mind makes this difficult. The intuition of Being is of a different order than intellectual analysis.

Throughout the day there are many fleeting moments of No-thought, even for those who are completely unconscious. Even those who identify with the voices in their heads have *brief stoppages* in their mental activity. Learning how to *stretch* these gaps in thinking is the key to becoming more present. Only in Presence - in the Space of No-thought, No-mind - can true Joy, Peace and Wisdom be found.

Suicide can be understood as an attempt to disidentify with the voices in our heads. Yet, we need not take our own lives to transcend the craziness in our minds. We need simply to *take note* of the misery created by our thoughts to escape their doom and gloom. Expand the blessed Respite of Presence and we will have entered the Kingdom of God.

The experience of hell is permitted by God in order to bring us to heaven. That is, when the pain of holding on becomes greater than the pain of letting go, we let go. Letting go of mind-made suffering opens the gates to Paradise.

Resting in God means cultivating an interior Space of silence and stillness where we listen to the power of Being. It is the hidden place of Letting go (*Gelassenheit*), of Acceptance, surrender, dispossession, Relinquishment and detachment. It is also the place of Openness, alert Attentiveness, virginal Receptivity and unalloyed Acceptance. It is the place of Presence: Presence to the present moment, regardless of what form the present moment takes. It is the Space of Presence, Wisdom and Love.

A sense of Presence is the sense of Being. It is an intuition of the miraculous fact that there is something rather than nothing. It is *astonishment* at the reality of Existence.

Life has no opposite. Death is not the opposite of life. Death and life are synonyms for the same Mystery. Death is life, and life is death. When we let go, we are lifted up. When we relinquish, we receive. When we surrender, we overcome.

Death is an event that happens only in Presence. Death is not the end of Presence but only a further affirmation of it.

Practicing Presence involves cultivating a certain intentional interior Emptiness which is nevertheless filled with alert Attentiveness. It is maintaining a sense of Spaciousness within - an unadulterated orientation of Openness and Acceptance in which even the fact of death is allowed to be.

The power of this unrestricted Acceptance is affirmation that death is an illusion of the mind. Thus, the power of Presence precedes and exceeds all that appears within it, including the fact of death. Once in touch with this Presence, the fear of death dissolves.

Presence itself is a form of living death. It is death to the ego and life to the spirit. 'Being here' for the other means we have, at least momentarily, 'died' to ourselves, i.e., to our ego. Being present is a form of *life in death*.

Presence is a place of Poise. When we are poised, we are devoid of thinking, yet filled with an alert Attentiveness. We have no agenda or expectations. We are ready to move right, left, or just remain still. Presence is a place of intense Listening. It is a Space of expectant Waiting. It is an Emptiness filled with unlabeled yet unequaled Anticipation.

The permanency we seek, beyond the world of appearing and disappearing forms, is found only in the experience of Presence. 'We are' and 'they are': this is the unchangeable reality amidst the kaleidoscopic flux of mental and physical objects. Seek your Peace in Presence rather than in the world of things.

Peace arises as possessiveness recedes. Joy abides when justifications cease. Serenity appears when struggling is abandoned. There is no difference between these terms. Wherever there is one, there is always the other. Self-surrender (death) and self-realization (life/resurrection) are, at bottom, identical.

'Looking' and 'Letting be' are key practices in learning how to be present. Presence is the power of Allowing, the power of Beholding. It makes nothing happen but simply allows what is to be. A hands-off approach to reality. The joy of sitting still.

Presence is thoughtless Awareness. It is consciousness *beyond cognition.* Presence is awareness of the Absolute. Intellection is limited to the contingent, the relative, the conditional, the finite. Presence is a participation in the Infinite.

Presence is a dynamic of perpetual Letting go (*Gelassenheit*), of self-emptying (*Kenosis*). It is a participation in the Life of God which is the creative Power of Letting Go (*Gelassenheit*) that says of all creation, '*Let it be...*' (cf. Gen. 1:3).

Letting be and Letting go are symbiotic, if not identical. They create that beautiful Space of ever-expanding Allowing, Welcoming, Accepting and Receiving. They are at once the conditions and fruits of Presence.

At the core of our *being there* is a radical Openness that is both our true identity *and* the Presence of God. Awareness of this Openness is our salvation, resulting in immediate Bliss.

Life forms arise and dissolve in our Awareness in an unceasing kaleidoscopic flow, but our capacity for Awareness precedes and succeeds them. Our personal Presence is untouched by the objects that appear and disappear in it. Our *noticing* of this fact affirms the transcendental nature of Presence.

In dying, many people become aware of Presence as if for the first time. As death approaches, the prospect of an eternal pregnant Pause arises in which some persons freshly discover their own transcendental selfhood. With this Apprehension, the Peace of God permeates their being.

Ultimately, death, life, and Presence are dimensions of the same Mystery. This is the Mystery of Mystical Nothingness: the Absolute Emptiness of Letting Be that is the Source and Summit of all that is.

'God' is the Mystery that makes the experience of Presence possible. 'God' is greater than the Mystery of Presence that God makes possible. God constitutes our own being *as* Presence, and in that Presence discloses God's-self as our transcendent and immanent Source.

Death is a reality only for the ego. In reality there is no death. In Presence, we experience death as another opportunity - perhaps our greatest opportunity - to practice Surrender. Whenever we surrender our mental hold on things, the truth of Reality sets us free.

The goodness of God, of Life, can only be *felt*. It cannot be experienced in thought. The Presence of God - the Source of our capacity to be present (knowingly conscious) - is tacitly experienced the more we cultivate a sense of Spaciousness within us.

Knowledge of God is always oblique, tacit, untoward. It is an Awareness given implicitly, much the way in which negative Space makes itself known in a work of art. God is present as the uncapturable *Background* of whatever is in the foreground. There is no possible way of making God a foreground Object. God is never an object. Knowledge of God is always given as the *unthematic Background* allowing all objects to appear.

Remaining still, Listening, cultivating sustained attentive Awareness without agenda - these are ways of accessing an intuitive experience of God. Every act of spacious Awareness momentarily suspends the action of the ego, opening us to the silent Ground of Being.

Life in the spirit means cultivating a sense of 'space consciousness.' Life in the ego means cultivating 'object awareness.'[6] It is in the Space *between thoughts* in which the Presence of God can be experienced. It is in the Pause, the Disruption, the Stop where the Presence of God is most likely to be discovered.

Where is 'God' to be found? In the Space of the 'time out,' the Space of the 'deep breath,' the Space of 'letting go,' the Space of non-attachment. Surrender and *Relinquishment* are the fertile soil for growing our Awareness of God.

*Dis-identification* with any and every thought we can have about anything or anyone is the path to salvation.

Indulging the ego is sacred violence. It assaults the spirit and crushes the soul, all in the name of personal fulfillment.

Ego is personal identification with the objects of our minds. We are not identical with the ideas we have about ourselves. We are not identical with the stories we tell about ourselves. We are not the picture of ourselves that we have in our heads. Still less are we the persons other people believe us to be. We are the those who are able to *recognize* that we *elude all the labels* that can be applied to us.

---

[6] Terms borrowed from the writings of Eckhart Tolle.

Emptiness, or Spaciousness, is at the heart of all things. Being is inherently transcendent, since all things are contingent and un-self-sustaining. Things can never provide their own explanation. Everything that exists comes from the *No-thing-ness* we call 'God.' God is the Mystery of Ineffability that makes possible the *is-ing-ness* of things. The Mystery of 'God' has no being, as we experience being.

God *is*, but not in the same manner as we *are*. We have *'existence,'* but God has no existence as we understand existence. Our existence *derives from* whatever it is that constitutes the Mystery of God. God is without - and beyond - being. Nevertheless, God *is* (cf. Ex. 3:14).

# 5th

## Wicker Basket

Evil is possible only where self-awareness is lacking. Or better: the only real evil is remaining unaware of one's capacity for Awareness. In our deceived ignorance, we trade our transcendent birthright for a pottage of the world's misery (cf. Gen. 25:34).

There are no problems for those who offer no resistance to the form of the present moment. Presence is the permanent insulation against the raging storms caused by mental turmoil.

The violence that results from the clashes of the world's polarities serves as a blessed invitation to return to Presence. In this view, there is no evil other than not seeing the polarities for what they are.

The world of objects is the world of polarization: north-south, east-west, up-down, over-under, male-female, Democrat-Republican, etc. Practicing Presence takes us out of the world of polarities into the Unity of Being. There, we discover ourselves one with, yet distinct from, the Source of all that is. Our lives are hidden with God in Presence.

There is no limit to the inner depths to which we can let go of our attachment to objects. It is important to notice that thoughts and feelings are nothing other than internal *objects*. Our ability to recognize them as such shows that our true nature transcends them and can never be fulfilled by identifying with them.

Allowing things to be exactly as they are in the present moment keeps us from losing ourselves in 'object consciousness.' It is in the Space of stepping back from whatever we perceive that true Wisdom is found and true seeing begins.

In the Space of Allowing, even the words of our worst enemies lose their power to harm us. Allowed to be, such words evaporate in the Space of Presence. The power of Acceptance dissolves all thrusts of aggression.

Without Space consciousness, reactivity is inevitable. Unless we can find the Pause, a knee-jerk reaction is likely. It is in the *gap between thoughts and action* where the possibility of Deliverance resides. To live in these Gaps is to be set free from the impulsiveness that is death to the spirit.

Objects in the world continually change and die. Acceptance of this fact brings immediate, and perhaps surprising, Peace. This Peace is an affirmation that we are not identical with our bodies and that who we are transcends both change and death.

Without Awareness, persons are like wind chimes clanging in the breeze. They may make beautiful sounds but they cannot make music. The music of heaven is heard only when a person Awakens to the power of the present moment. Such is the place of Presence - the sacred Space in which the voices of angels resound.

*Philip Krill*

Eternal life is the Awareness and Appreciation of the Mystery that who we are is not identical with anything we see, do or think; rather, it partakes of the Infinite I AM who makes this Awareness possible.

Every time we single out the present instant as the focus of our undivided Attention, we are transported beyond time, into a Space where ego cannot operate. Attentiveness to the present moment is deliverance from suffering. It is the very definition of Love.

We can be happy anywhere because we can be present anywhere. One instant of Presence brings greater joy than a lifetime of achievement. Nothing satisfies the human person more than the experience of Presence. Persons who practice Presence are never imprisoned, even if they are in jail. We are only ever prisoners of our own thoughts. Presence takes us beyond thinking and sets us free.

Interior surrender often has external effects. It's as if the whole universe is benignly impacted when any person lets go of an egoic attachment that is causing personal suffering. It's as if the cosmos itself rejoices at the smallest act of internal Relinquishment.

Presence neutralizes the suffering that comes from experiencing the world as polarized. The world of form is a menagerie of polarities: east from west, up from down, good from bad, light from darkness, women from men, etc. In the experience of Presence, polarities are perceived for what they are, and thus overcome. A transcendent sense of Peace arises for as long as the dualities of the world are accepted without interpretation or objection.

Nothing appears in the world that does not emerge from an archetypal Wisdom beyond human intelligence. To see the world as a kaleidoscopic Unfolding of this Wisdom is to experience a Presence that is one with this same Wisdom.

The experience of Presence is the experience of Love - the Power that allows Being to be exactly as it is. Love is the attentive Acceptance of Reality that reveals all that is as beautiful.

To *notice* our thoughts is to rise above them. It is also to be relieved of the suffering they inevitably cause us.

We can't have our cake and eat it too. That is, we cannot desire to *possess* an object and to *love* it at the same time. We must relinquish our desire to possess in order to love. For to love is to simply be present to, and Presence is devoid of possessiveness. Covetousness kills love, while Presence saves.

The moment we move from simple Awareness to analysis, our capacity for Presence is compromised. It's like changing the focus of our attention while driving from the road ahead to the windshield: we are likely to crash and burn.

When we step back from our thoughts, we become aware of a Reality that both includes and transcends our ideas about it.

Trapped in thought, we feel imprisoned; *noticing* our imprisonment, we are set free. The question is: how long can we stay out of prison?

We seek in the past and the future that which can be had only in the present. Yet, nothing is ever really 'had,' even in the present. In Presence, everything is experienced as a Gift, which is why we call it 'the present.'

Detachment from our thoughts is perhaps the greatest accomplishment in life. It means the end of suffering and the beginning of eternal Joy. In Presence, we transcend time and Space. We experience ourselves as somehow *prior* to all that appears in our experience.

Conceptualization blinds us to the priority of pure Awareness. Learning to be present to the workings of our own minds frees us from their domination.

When we see reality through the screen of conceptualization, we see '*as through a glass darkly*' (cf. 1 Cor. 13:12). Mental configurations distort our experience of Reality.

Violence is made possible by our critical ideas of the other. If we could kill our *concepts* about other people, there would be no more violence in the world.

It is impossible to do evil in the Space of Presence. Presence is a Mystery of Availability in which no animosity or antagonism can survive. Presence is Love, and Love casts out all fear and mendacity (cf. 1 Jn. 4:18).

Expectations are premeditated resentments. Presence frees us from both. Presence allows us to see possibilities where before we could only see only potential problems.

In Presence, our problems momentarily disappear. The challenge is to remain so consistently in the Now that they disappear forever.

To *accept* is to transcend. To *notice* is to get beyond. To *acknowledge* is to defuse. To *embrace* is to disarm. The evils of argument and antagonism cannot endure the Presence of *non-resistance*.

We step out of the world of suffering the moment we *dis-identify* with our mental constructs. The Relief that comes from putting *distance* between ourselves and our thoughts about ourselves is immediate. It is also the Space in which Wisdom about what to do, or not to do, can arise. Wisdom does not come through intellectual analysis but only through Presence.

The 'intuition of Being' is obscured by 'object awareness.' The unanswered question always is: why is the something - anything - rather than nothing? Unless an intuitive sense of the *'is-ing-ness'* of things is given us, thinking generates dichotomies than inevitably become destructive.

Being (*Esse*) precedes and exceeds beings (*essentia*), yet it is manifest only in them. Things have no 'is-ing-ness' (being) without Being (*Esse*), but the Mystery of Being (*Esse*) is disclosed only in beings (*essentia*).

God is in the world, and the world is in God, but God is not the world, and the world is not God. The being (existence) of the world is a participation in the Being (*Esse*) of 'God,' while the Being (*Esse*) we call God is the unparticipateable *Source* of all that has being.

It is in the *Now* that a sense of Aliveness arises. The *immediacy of the moment* has the power to dissolve the objects of consciousness that threaten to obscure it. The key is Presence. When we are present to someone or something, we are *transported beyond the world of labels* into the timelessness of Being. Herein lies the Peace of God and the love of others.

Presence is at the epicenter of death, for Presence is the *death of the fear of death*. Once death is accepted as simply another event that arises and dissolves in the experience of Presence, it ceases to threaten us.

Experienced in Presence, death is a flower opening, a butterfly emerging. We rise from the tomb of ego identity when we die to our labeling and allow our mental constructs to decompose.

Being present means creating Space. Such Space is the Breath of the Holy Spirit. It is the Space of Allowing, the Breath of Beholding. The Spirit of God is so elusive because it is without agenda. It allows everything to be just as it is.

Letting-be-ness (*Gelassenheit*) is a synonym for the Presence of God. Letting-be-ness also points to the identity of what we call death and life. For to 'let go' is always a creative act. It actuates an Effulgence of Life that otherwise could not be. Death and life are not two sides of the same coin, but constitute a single Mystery at the heart of creation.

Another term for God's *Letting-go-ness* is *Kenosis*: self-emptying, self-dispossession.

From the infinite Nothingness of God's self-dispossessing Life explodes everything that is. Because God is eternally dying to Godself, the universe is continually expanding. The death of God within God is the life of the world.

Presence has the power to dissolve the past. Memories - good or bad - are incinerated in the fire of the present moment. The Power of Presence makes all things new (cf. Rev. 21:5).

All lesser loves - including those of family and friends (cf. Lk. 14:26; Mt. 19:27-28) - are rendered irrelevant in the experience of Presence. They are relativized to the point of nothingness. The experience of Presence makes whatever went before in our lives, or whatever may come after, appear as so much nothingness.

Our true identity is discovered in the sacred Space of Presence. Here, we participate in a Power greater than ourselves which is *also* the form and essence of what we are. We are not God, yet we are one *with* God *in* the Mystery of Presence.

Our minds cannot know themselves, just as our eyes cannot see themselves. Both enjoy a Light within that makes our knowing and seeing possible. That Light is Presence.

God is not identical with Presence, yet the experience of Presence affords our most immediate contact with God. Presence is the Self-communication of God. It is also the foundation and fulfillment of our existence as creatures of God.

The only words that matter are those that flow from Presence. Everything else rings hollow.

Words emerging from Presence have prophetic power resonating from them. They are of a fundamentally different order from conceptual explanations.

# 6th

## Wicker Basket

*Proclamation* is worlds apart from *explanation*. Presence expresses Itself in proclamation, thinking in explanation.

Ego contains the seeds of its own undoing. Insanity eventually subverts itself. Misery undermines misery by making itself unbearable. Suffering becomes the cure for suffering when it is accepted. Acceptance is the answer to all our problems today.[7]

Salvation - Enlightenment - is always Awakening from a nightmare of egoic thinking. Oh, what a relief to stop fighting ghosts!

Spiritual Awakening occurs when we *relax* into the present moment. Inner Peace arises when we stop fighting anything and anyone. Relief comes when we own the truth that we are exactly where we are meant to be; when we realize that the form of the present moment is nothing less than perfect.

Acceptance of the way things are is the only way to effect positive change. Nothing good can be forced. Things unfold according to a Higher Wisdom when we stop trying to push the river of Life. Here alone we find real Peace.

---

[7] One of the slogans of Alcoholics Anonymous.

When we live in the 'Space' of self-transcendence, everything around us loses its power to define us. Things are what they are, and we are who we are (cf. Ex. 3:14). Realizing this truth is the key to happiness.

Those who are consciously self-transcendent realize their Being does not come from themselves. They also recognize that they do not belong completely to themselves. There is a Power greater than us that is both present *within* and *beyond* us. This Power we sometimes call 'God.' 'God' can be neither located nor described. Yet, the Power of God, like the Mystery of Presence, is as undeniable as it is indefinable.

Presence is a *Light* in which all objects are seen. Presence makes our perceptions possible but is Itself unaffected by all that appears within it.

The Power of *Presence* and the Power of the *Now* are distinct but inseparable. The Power of the Now is the Presence of God making itself felt in the experience of self-transcendence.

Memories are thoughts that dissolve in the uncreated Light of Presence. The Light of Presence is the rising sun that causes the mists of our minds to evaporate, leaving only a crystalline vision of the Beauty of creation.

The present moment is the time of God's salvation. Everything is continually redeemed in the Power of the Now.

Addiction is identification with an object of the mind. Such attachments are illusions, but not realized as such until they have inflicted massive suffering. The good news is, once the suffering becomes unbearable, Deliverance becomes possible.

Addiction is overcome when Awareness arises. When we become *aware* that we are miserable we are, in that moment of Awareness, no longer miserable. Recovery from addiction involves expanding the moment of misery Awareness. When this happens, our failures become the means of our salvation, our weaknesses become our ways of Awakening to our true lives.

The experience of Presence begins when we are aware of ourselves as the *Observers of ourselves.* In that moment, we realize, not that there are two of us, but that our selfhood is self-transcendent. We are *capable* of becoming aware of ourselves. Thus, we are inherently oriented to going above and beyond ourselves, while remaining wholly ourselves and within ourselves. This experience of transcendent Selfhood is the key to understanding everything in life and entering the Kingdom of God. God is the *Source* of our capacity for self-transcendence.

The Power of Presence shows itself as we strive to live more and more continuously as our own internal Observers. That is to say, the more we are aware of ourselves as the *Witnesses* of ourselves - the more we are 'present' to ourselves - the more we are 'established' in Presence. Contemplative prayer is a matter of constantly refreshing the internal witness within us.

In the *Kena Upanishad* we read: '*Not that which the mind knows, but that by which the mind knows. Not that which the eye sees, but that by which the eye sees. Not that which the ear hears, but that by which the ear hears…*'. God is the '*that by which.*'

Religion is what people do before Awakening to the Power of Presence. Becoming aware of the *priority of Awareness* is the end of religion. To learn how to live in Presence is the purpose of all religious practice.

Awakening means being *arrested* by the fact *that* things exist, not *what* or *how* things exist. The experience of Presence and the '*intuition of Being*' always occur together. It is also an experience of being surprised by Joy.

In our Awareness of Awareness, we sense that God and we are one, yet still distinct. Awakened by Presence as a Power greater than ourselves, we experience ourselves as both real and nothing simultaneously.

In Presence, our personal uniqueness is not dissolved but perfected. Yet, this uniqueness remains hidden, even to us. '*Our lives are hidden with Christ* (Presence) *in God*' (cf. Col. 3:3).

The experience of Presence is perpetually New. It refreshes Itself from moment to moment. Presence is the Power of the Now. In Presence '*we live and move and have our being*' (cf. Acts 17:28).

Consciousness is not an Ocean in which we disappear like a drop of water, or from which we arise like one of its waves. Consciousness is our *participation in* an Awareness that precedes and makes possible our own.

The experience of Presence begins as a momentary Flash of recognition. It's as if the Power of the present moment makes itself felt as infinitely more Real than our memories of the past or fears of the future. It is as if the transcendent nature of our personal selfhood reveals itself to Itself.

Presence is an aware Availability without agenda. Presence is filled with Openness but empty of analysis. Presence is Attentiveness without interpretation.

Presence is an intuitive Awareness of the Condition for its own possibility. It is the realization that the Source of Awareness is greater than the self.

Presence is a Mystery of undefended Openness. It is the opposite of unthinking superiority. Presence is devoid of judgment, criticism, skepticism or angst. It is the indefinable Space of Love.

In Presence, time disappears. There is only the Now. There is no waiting around for something to happen. Presence is the Inscape of all that is happening Now.

Presence recognizes perceptions as egoic projections. Presence never judges a book by its cover, nor persons by their personae. Presence intuits the capacity for Spaciousness within the other. Presence reverences the other as one with Itself.

In Presence, there is neither male nor female, neither gay nor straight, neither good nor bad. In Presence, bifurcations and antinomies are unknown. At the same time, *distinctiveness* is acknowledged and appreciated, differences are celebrated and embraced. The *alterity* of the other is seen as an invitation to intimacy, not as an occasion for alienation. Presence is a Space of union where differentiation is both respected and perfected.

Presence is the antidote to the insanity of the ego. Ego is the unobserved mind. Presence is the empty Container that deprives thinking of its oxygen. When our thoughts die down, the Power of Presence arises.

It seems like a miracle when, in Presence, we are no longer waiting for the next thing to happen. We are able to watch the world go by without being drawn into its melodrama.

We escape the totalitarianism of oppressive thinking when Presence alights within us. Actual concentration camps come about when the world's best and brightest do not know how to cultivate Presence.

In Presence, there is nowhere to get to. We are already there. Some call this place 'the kingdom of God.'

Presence is of infinite Depth. It encompasses *us*, not us it. We are partakers of a Self-consciousness that makes our own self-transcendence possible. Some call this Self-consciousness 'God.'

*Sat, Chit, Ananda*: Being, Consciousness, Bliss. This is the trinitarian Mystery also known as Presence.

Thoughts are like petulant children. Their childish whining is silenced with adult Awareness. When thoughts, like children, know they are being watched, they usually behave better.

There is a place for thoughts in Presence, but only if they arise from *inspiration* not *aspiration*. Presence inspires creative thinking, thinking impedes creativity.

Thoughts are like pieces of furniture, and Presence is like a room in which these pieces are placed. Presence remains as unaffected by the thoughts that arise within It as does a room by the furniture it contains.

We remain spiritually somnambulant when our Awareness is confined to objects. It's our capacity to *go beyond* object-consciousness that brings us Presence and Peace.

In Presence, a person is never at the mercy of circumstances. Victimhood is abolished in Presence. There is only Light, Gratitude, and Joy.

In Presence we know the truth of Lovelace's poem, *'Stone walls do not a prison make, nor iron bars a cage ...'* Presence makes mental and emotional imprisonment impossible.

Presence begins and ends with Acceptance: of ourselves, of others, of every present moment, just as it is. In the Space of Acceptance, the promises of the Serenity Prayer come true: *'God, grant me the serenity to accept the things I cannot change, the courage to change the things I can, and the Wisdom to know the difference.'*

Life is filled with many satisfactions: eating, drinking, embracing, playing, achieving, etc. *Noticing* these satisfactions *without identifying with them* brings even greater Satisfaction. This is the *Bliss* of Presence, which precedes - and exceeds - all earthly joys.

Love of enemies is possible in Presence. Presence dissolves our antipathies, while increasing our Acuity of discernment. It makes us *'wise as serpents but as innocent as doves'* (cf. Mt. 10:16). Presence makes us aware of evil but keeps us from being bitten by it.

Presence makes every moment perfect. It also perfects the persons who abide in it. Presence is the power of God's deification of our lives. Presence is an immediate participation in the Life of God.

# 7th
# Wicker Basket

Presence is contagious. When we live in Presence, those who come into *our* presence are affected by it. Presence is healing. Presence brings Peace. The Peace of God is communicated to others through us.

Who hasn't heard a mother saying to a child in distress, *'Everything's going to be OK.'*? In Presence we discover the ultimate *OK-ness* of things. We realize that nothing can happen that is not redeemed by Presence.

Presence convinces us of what Julian of Norwich famously said: *'All shall be well, all shall be well, and all manner of things shall be well ...'*[8]

Presence is not to be confused with passivity. It is just the opposite. Presence is an alert Attentiveness in which prudent action is made possible by the Wisdom that arises within it. Because it comes from a place of equanimous Poise, such action is without the passion that would otherwise defeat it. The enjoyment of any activity comes not from the activity itself but from the Presence with which we engage in it. This is because Presence involves a certain *forgetfulness of thinking*. In Presence, our minds may be working, but they are doing so energized within a larger and more diffuse field of Attentiveness. Concentration is a manifestation of Presence in which thinking has a real, yet subordinate, role.

---

[8] *Revelations of Divine Love.*

Presence is found in the Pause. It can be sensed at the apogee or nadir of every movement. T. S. Eliot called it '*the still point of the turning world. Neither flesh nor fleshless; neither from nor towards; at the still point, there the dance is, but neither arrest nor movement. And do not call it fixity, where past and future are gathered. Neither movement from nor towards, neither ascent nor decline. Except for the point, the still point, there would be no dance, and there is only the dance.*'[9]

Thomas Merton also knew the power of the Still Point: '*At the center of our being is a point of nothingness which is untouched by sin and by illusion, a point of pure truth, a point or spark which belongs entirely to God, which is never at our disposal, from which God disposes of our lives, which is inaccessible to the fantasies of our own mind or the brutalities of our own will. This little point of nothingness and of absolute poverty is the pure glory of God in us … It is in everybody, and if we could see it we would see these billions of points of light coming together in the face and blaze of a sun that would make all the darkness and cruelty of life vanish completely*'.[10]

Presence is that indefinable Space from which creation continually comes, the Still Point wherein existence finds its Beginning and End (cf. Rev. 22:13).

Our lives are like celluloid images of a film, brought to life by a Light behind them. That Light is the *Light of Presence* emanating from the Mystery of God.

---

[9] T.S. Eliot, *Burnt Norton* in *Four Quartets.*

[10] Thomas Merton, *Conjectures of a Guilty Bystander.*

Presence, in a certain way, is a synonym for God. Yet, in truth, God is unknowable, except as the ineffable Source of what we experience as Presence.

To be 'born again' means to continually face forward, letting the past be past, and living completely in the Now. In the Space of the Now, everything is continually fresh, filled with New Life. Living completely in the Now, we always experience life as a Gift, never as a burden.

Only the Now is real. In the Present moment, *timing* replaces time as the measure of Meaning. Every moment of *chronos* becomes an opportunity for *kairos*.

Phrases like, '*Don't lose touch with yourself,*' '*I wish I hadn't been so stupid!*,' or '*If I had it to over again...*' reveal the ubiquity of Presence and our capacity for self-transcendence. Our ability to be present to ourselves is of a piece with the Presence of God within us. This is what St. Augustine meant when he said that God is '*higher than our highest and more inward than our innermost self*' (*interior intimo meo et superior summo meo*).[11]

Presence doesn't need words to communicate Itself to others. If a picture is worth a thousand words, then a single glance of Presence is enough to change the world.

---

[11] *Confessions*, III, 6, 11.

Words have no power detached from Presence. Without Presence, a person speaking is *'a noisy gong or a clanging cymbal'* (1 Cor. 13:1).

Living in Presence has certain physical manifestations, chief among them being 'soft eyes'. Soft eyes, open heart. Neither can be deliberately willed. Or, if they can, they will always have a robotic atonality about them. No, truly soft eyes come as a by-product of a deep, interior Surrender to the Power of Presence.

Presence is a drama-free zone. Histrionics lose their steam in Presence, like a bullet shot underwater.

Just as water is stronger than steel, Presence is stronger than the objects that inhabit it. Living in Presence, nothing can harm us, and fear disappears (cf. Rom. 8:28; 1 Jn. 4:16).

Living knowingly in Presence is something that must be achieved again and again, moment by moment. As a transcendental Apprehension, Presence is both a Gift and a task. Awakening is becoming aware of our inherent nature as Awareness, but in an *unceasing* way. This requires an effort that is difficult to describe but clear in experience. Enlightenment is not a one-time event. It needs *perpetual refreshing*. One does this by becoming ever more aware of the Source of Awareness, both within and beyond one's self.

Enlightenment - or living in Presence - is making a *permanent shift* from analysis to Attention. It is to continually rise above the activity of the mind. It is to put the mind into neutral, so it doesn't overheat. It is to recognize that our *Awareness* of a thing is not itself a thing; that our *Consciousness* of a thought is not itself a thought; that our *Observation* of an emotion is not an emotion. Enlightenment is a *perpetual rising above* our thoughts and emotions such that those thoughts and motions are seen for what they are: non-substantial objects that have no power to affect us. Enlightenment is Freedom, establishing us in a Blissful Awareness that disarms our fears, doubts, and insecurities.

Presence is the experience of pure Actuality. In Presence, the *is-ing-ness* of things is so palpably apprehended that we are rendered mute in wordless wonder.

Though Presence is characterized by supreme equanimity, it is not stoic indifference. On the contrary, it is perfect Bliss (*Ananda*). Speaking of this state of Presence, Meister Eckhart says, '*When we are correctly translated into the divine being, God becomes mind as well as everything God has ... This means that all anxiety is cast out of our hearts, so that in our hearts there be nothing but constant joy ... and even if we had to see with our own eyes our father and all our friends killed, our hearts would not be moved by it ... for when we are translated into the divine being, suffering has no place, since in God there is neither wrath nor grief, but only love and joy.*'[12]

Thinking can no sooner attain to Presence than Sherlock Holmes can find Arthur Conan Doyle.

---

[12] *Collected Sermons.*

Suffering is always a symptom of too much thinking. It can also serve as a portal to Presence, if it triggers our Awareness that thinking is our problem.

Perhaps the greatest achievement in life is to learn how to stop thinking. In the Space of the Stop, Wisdom arises.

Presence is the infinite Horizon within which thoughts appear. Thoughts themselves are unaware of the Horizon that makes their appearance possible.

Ego is the insane thinking that restricts itself to thoughts instead of averting to the infinite Background of Presence from which they arise and to which they return.

The radical refusal to harbor thoughts is an important step to living in Presence. Recognizing this Refusal itself as a manifestation of Presence is a way to enter more deeply into Presence.

Presence is beyond words, yet the experience of Presence has a certain communicability which flows from the experience itself. Though it is impossible to capture the experience of Presence and transpose it integrally into objectifying concepts, it remains nevertheless the case that without this reflection, Presence would remain unrecognizable.

Though Presence and thinking are of different orders - i.e., Background to foreground - they can peacefully co-exist and are almost always found together. And, even if it were possible to clear the foreground of our lives of all thinking and live contemplatively in the Background of Presence - even then, Presence would manifest Itself as an infinite, receding Background, behind which, or into which, we can never fully get. In short, Presence is a transcendental Mystery, implicitly known in every act of thinking, but captured neither by thinking nor the elimination of thought.

Presence is always greater than our efforts to understand it. It is a Mystery that is at once the Source of our existence and the Horizon toward which we are eternally drawn.

Presence is the manifestation of the Eternal in us, and also of a Mystery greater than ourselves. We are in God, and God is in us, but we are not God, and God is not us. In Presence, we experience our *co-inherence* - not our identity - with God.

Presence follows us like a shadow. It eludes our every effort to grasp it. We have to grasp Presence *intuitively*, if we are to grasp it at all.

Presence approaches like a shy, elusive lover. It flees our direct gaze and will not give itself to any ham-fisted paramour.

Most people know what it means to 'be present.' Few people recognize this experience as the Presence of God.

The Mystery of Presence is always experienced as a fresh Discovery. It is an 'intuition of Being' that interrupts and arrests egoic consciousness. It is the power of Actuality breaking through the mists of mentation. It is the miracle of Awareness showing our cognition to be its step-child.

Rooted in the Space of the Now, we are sitting in the lap of Presence. There is nothing to be done except enjoy its Embrace.

A good question to ask at any moment: *'Are we friendly or hostile to what is?'*. To prefer *'what is not'* or *'what was'* or *'what could be'* or *'what might be'* to *'what is'* is to be spiritually dead. The Infinity of Being manifests itself only to those who embrace the finitude of the present moment.

One's experience of time is a function of one's degree of Presence. When we are present, time flies. When we are not present, time drags on forever.

All perceptions are distortions of the truth until they are brought into the redemptive Space of Presence. When we are *present without judgment*, we can see things as they *are*, not as we would like them to be. In which case we are in a better position to address them wisely, which often means letting them be and doing nothing at all.

Presence 'miniaturizes' our sense of what we can or should do in any situation. In Presence, we see that one small seed of action coming from Presence is more powerful than a lifetime of activity unconnected to Presence.

In Presence we see all men and women as brothers and sisters. The need for political correctness vanishes. The language of social reform and/or self-improvement becomes meaningless. The truth that all persons are one with us is self-evident in the experience of Presence. We realize we are sisters and brothers because we have the same Progenitor in Presence.

Presence is the fulcrum on the teeter-totter between past and future - that indefinable Still Point of complete Emptiness which can effortlessly balance the weight of the world. Presence is the Archimedean Point upon which the entire universe rests, lighter than a feather.

Everything becomes unbearably heavy when thinking begins. There is never enough time to figure things out, everything seems unfinished, satisfaction eludes us. The moment we shift into Presence, however, life begins to move in slow motion. We are able to *respond*, not react, to *contemplate* rather than cogitate, to view things with the *soft eyes* of the beholder in lieu of the cold stare of the analyst. Why go back to the burden of problem-solving after experiencing the sapiential Bliss of Presence?

Presence is approached only asymptotically.[13] Presence is the Vanishing Point which gives perspective to our world but is not of this world. Presence is the Zero Point of our existence, making everything possible while remaining Nothing in itself.

Presence is the Apex of everything that arises - the indefinable Apogee which draws all things out of nothingness, in which all things are unified and converge, yet which in itself is ungraspable and known only in thoughtless wonder.

---

[13] An asymptote of a curve is a line which is tangent to the curve at a point at infinity.

# 8th

## Wicker Basket

Presence preserves and perfects *particularity*. Personal identity is not dissolved in Presence but affirmed as partaking, in a unique way, in a Power greater than itself.

*Theosis* - or deification - takes place in Presence. The longer we remain in Presence, the more indistinguishable from God we become. In *Theosis*, God remains God, and we remain ourselves, but we are also transfigured with the Mystery of Presence that God is.

In Presence, death is revealed to be an illusion. To enter Presence, we must 'die' to every movement within us other than the act of Letting go (*Gelassenheit*). But the act of Letting go is the inner meaning of 'death.' And since every act of Letting go results in inner Peace and a spiritual lifting up, death is revealed to be as but a manifestation of a person coming fully alive. We are most fully alive when we have let go completely. That is, when we have discovered 'death' is the key to, indeed is synonymous with, Life.

We haven't begun to live until we have discovered that for which we would happily die. Our willingness to let go of life brings us to the threshold of eternal Life. To step over this threshold, we must Awaken to the fact that it is our *willingness* to die - not the object for which we are willing to give our lives - that is the Source of our fearlessness and Love.

Fear of death dissolves in the Space of Presence. This is because past and future cease to have meaning. A Fulness (*Pleroma*) of Being is revealed as a Mystery synonymous with the Power of the Now. It is perfect Peace, Serenity, and Life. Once there, we never want to be anywhere else. Presence is heaven on earth.

Fear of death *is* death. Fear is life unaware of itself and therefore dead to the only thing that makes life worth living - the power of Presence. Conversely, life in Presence means death to everything but the Life of the Now. This death to the fear of death is what religious people call eternal Life.

Abiding in Presence, we also project Presence. The Power of Presence extends outward from the person practicing Presence to the furthest reaches of the cosmos. A single moment in Presence does more to heal the universe than a lifetime of good works or social action.

Thinking diminishes the projective Power of Presence. Thinking functions as a kind of spiritual Faraday cage, greatly impeding the radiant impact of Presence.

The greatest thing we can do in life is to know how to enter Presence and stay there. There is no other Activity that can so fulfill a human being.

Experiencing Presence and abiding in Presence is not a vocation separate from any career path. Practicing Presence is compatible with every activity we undertake. Not only compatible, but whenever we are fully present, ego disappears and both us and what we are doing are perfected by the Power of Presence.

Knowing how to find and practice Presence is what the bible calls *'finding the pearl of great price'* (Mt. 13:46). This hidden treasure is worth more than everything else in the world, including country, family, and friends (cf. Lk. 14:26).

Presence is what makes science possible, not something science can ever unearth.

Those who abide in Presence know the nothingness of the world. Not that created things do not exist, or are unimportant, but there exists no conceivable comparison between the things of this world and the experience of Presence. They also know that Presence can have no conceivable biological, chemical, or other physiological origin, even though the experience of Presence manifests itself in bodily and neurological impulses that can be observed and measured.

Cognition - thinking - goes out of itself towards objects. Its focus is other than itself. *Self-aware cognition* makes *itself* an object of its own intentionality. This is a huge step forward, since it is thinking aware of itself. Yet, 'thinking about thinking' is still an exercise in cognition, not the transcendental experience of Presence. Thinking about thinking is not the same as experiencing thinking as an *epiphany* of a Knowingness that is both prior to and generative of the operations of reason and perception. Cognition, in other words, is ontologically unable to grasp the conditions of its own possibility.

Time is synonymous with thought. Our capacity for Presence is the secret passage to eternity, hidden in plain sight.

There is always something missing for those who identify with the mind. Thought-identification prevents us from living in Presence. Utopian thinking masks the underlying misery of those incarcerated by their thoughts.

Nothing is right with the world when our mental obsession with past or future keeps us from experiencing the Joy of the present moment. Looking for the kingdom of God on earth or in heaven, we miss the kingdom of God *within* us (cf. Lk. 17:21).

Unaware of the Source of its own frustration, the mind doubles down on its efforts to discover the secrets of life through analysis. The mind, blind to the limits and the transcendent Source of its own operations, is like a dog chasing its tail unto exhaustion.

The world of time and Space exists to *frustrate* our desire to know and control it. The mind exists to reveal its own self-insufficiency. Everything in this world is a Source of *unfulfilled desire* until such time as we Awaken to our generative place within the world as Presence.

Before the Big Bang, we were, because Presence is.

We enter Presence when we catch a glimpse of the *sheer is-ing-ness* of things. Usually this is a fleeting Awareness - a sudden Encounter with *the enigma of Being*, an arresting Intuition of the *sheer unexpectedness* of any thing, an Awareness of the perfect immediacy, the *utter uncanniness* of Reality. This 'intuition of Being' is like being stopped in our tracks by the inexplicable power of Actuality. It is the surprising Awareness that 'what is' has no necessary connection with the fact '*that* it is.' It is the existential realization that no existent thing can account for its own Actuality. This intuition is followed by an abiding Amazement at the gratuity of Being, as well as the realization that our minds can never grasp the Source of our own amazement. This Source is Presence.

Persons living in Presence have learned how to cultivate a sense of the *startling fortuity* of all that is. They abide in a continuous state of *joyous wonder* that every dimension of contingent reality, including their own minds, is completely lacking in any mark of inherent necessity or self-sufficiency. Such persons remain perpetually and delightfully surprised by the *unexpected 'there-ness'* of things. They are strangely elated by their awareness that *nothing contains the ground of its own existence.* They sense that 'all that is' derives, at every instant, from a Source 'outside' itself. Yet, they also realize that there is no 'outside' or 'inside' to Whatever-it-is that makes their perception of 'outside' and 'inside' possible. This kind of Wakefulness is habitual only in those who have discovered Presence as the Source of their, and the world's, existence.

Presence annihilates guilt and shame. Presence renders our moral calculus superfluous. Presence reveals true Freedom to be something *beyond* freedom of choice. Persons in Presence awaken to a Splendor beyond principles or predilections. Persons in Presence are in possession of a Beauty *in which* all things are experienced as perfect in their unrepeatable Actuality. For such persons there is nothing left to desire other than the prolonged Joy of basking in *the gracious needlessness of Being.*

For persons in Presence, *freedom* is *not* the ability to weigh and choose among options. It is their very *inability* to desire anything other than remaining in ecstatic Awareness of the gratuity of Being. Such persons are completely free, perfectly content to abide in the infinite Horizon of meaning that makes knowing and doing possible. This ungraspable Horizon is Presence.

Presence is the Power of God making itself known as a Mystery of personal *there-for-you-ness.* Presence is the manifestation of Divine Personhood.

Presence unifies, thinking divides. Awareness allows, analysis forbids. Acceptance receives, evaluation excludes. Presence hides wherever interpretation appears.

The human mind can be a torture chamber for those who do not know how to transcend their own thinking. Constant analysis is an exercise in *negative transcendence.* It is a search for truth by *tearing things apart.* Such subdivision proceeds *ad infinitum* until it arrives, not at the truth, but in mental futility. Such futility, however, can also awaken us to Presence if it is seen and accepted for what it is.

Thinking partakes of Presence when it perceives the beauty of creation *without commentary*.

Thinking and Presence are not opposites. Presence is *ontologically prior* to thinking, just as Being is ontologically prior to *beings*. Thinking takes place *within* Presence, but Presence has no intrinsic connection with thinking. Thinking imbued with Presence is Wisdom. Thinking which mistakes itself *for* Presence is called insanity.

Presence plays hide-and-seek with our thoughts. It shows itself in fleeting glimpses amidst the forest of ideas that grows in our minds. Only when the forest is perfectly still, does Presence come out to play.

Problems and thought are inseparable. No thoughts, no problems. The trick is learning how to be supremely Aware *without thinking*.

Presence functions like noise-cancelling headphones: It eliminates the background noise, allowing our spirits to hear the silent music of Being.

We are in Presence and Presence is in us but we are not identical. Nor are we simply an instance of Presence manifesting itself. It doesn't work that way.

It is impossible not to be aware of ourselves in the experience of Presence. Even when translucent with Presence, we remain uniquely ourselves, but empty of ego.

We are made in the image and likeness of Presence, but we are not identical with the Source of our own identity. We are *one* with Presence, but in an irreducibly *derivative* way. Presence and we are one, but Presence is always *greater* than us. We are they who are, *in* the One who is I AM.

We speak of Presence as a noun, but we experience it as a verb. In this way, Presence and 'God' are alike. For to experience Presence is to apprehend the Source of our own existence as one with, yet greater than, ourselves. It is a personal Encounter with a Power both *within* and *greater than* ourselves.

Our experience of Presence perfects, rather than dissolves, our sense of personal identity. It shows each of us to be a unique, irreducible, unsubstitutable dwelling place for Presence.

In Presence, we realize that personal identity and ego are not identical. We realize that to be who we are does not threaten the I AM from whom and for whom we are made.

In Presence we are at once *more* ourselves and *less* ourselves. That is, more our *true* selves and less our *egoic* selves.

In Presence, distinctions do not disappear; they simply no longer appear as *adversarial*. That is, *otherness* is still recognized, but not experienced as a Source of *opposition*. *Differences* are still seen, but not as occasions for *antagonism*. Estrangement and alienation are gone, while differentiation is perfected and made peaceful.

As the quintessential Mystery of transcendence, Presence is indefinable. It exceeds our ability to describe it, much less possess it. It is not an *'it.'* To try to say it *is*, betrays it. Yet, Presence can easily be experienced. It is experienced in every act of Letting go (*Gelassenheit*).

Presence is experienced in every act of perception, but only as the *Background* of what is perceived. As such, this Background can never be fully brought into focal awareness. It always remains the unseen *Horizon* of that which appears in our field of our perception.

We say Presence is inherently *transcendental*, incapable of being known or described in the usual ways, because, as the Background of every foreground, it always *recedes* from our attempts to bring it into focused awareness. To expand our vision beyond the foreground to include the background is simply to establish a larger, more diffusive Background. Which is to say, once any background becomes a foreground, another Background is immediately constellated that reveals the previous one as relative. If we expand this dynamic *ad infinitum*, we catch a glimpse of the transcendental nature of Presence.

Another image for the elusive nature of Presence is that of the Horizon. The closer one gets to any horizon, the further it recedes. Presence is the Horizon beyond all horizons which gives every horizon its irresistible allure.

A sense of Presence readily arises through inner *body awareness*. In such Awareness, mental projections are momentarily withdrawn, and a felt sense of Relief and Peace appears. This is the power of Presence, the Bliss of the Now.

# 9th

# Wicker Basket

There is an invisible, *Virginal Point* of Presence within every person that can be imagined as functioning like the center of gravity of any object.[14] It's at once within and beyond us. Through this invisible Virginal Point we receive our inner coherence and stability.

Those who intentionally practice being present experience Presence as a Reality that both *precedes* and *exceeds* their own being. They know Presence *has* them, not that *they* possess Presence. At the same time, they sense that it somehow 'pleases' Presence to manifest Itself in their acts of being present. In some sense, Presence *depends on* practitioners of Presence to awaken others to the reality and power of Presence.

It is not necessarily a matter of sustaining a sense of Presence for as long as possible. It is more a matter of *returning again and again* to the *Power* of Presence when we *notice* ourselves lost in thought. The measure of true Enlightenment, if there be such a thing, is *how often,* not how long, we return to Presence.

'*Noticing*' is the quickest and perhaps most frequent means for entering Presence. When we *notice* we are not present, we are once again present. When we *notice* we are getting anxious, we are, in the noticing, no longer anxious. When we *notice* we are over-thinking things, we are no longer over-thinking them. No matter how momentarily, whenever we *take note* of what we are doing, we transcend ourselves and enter the Space of Presence. In this Space of *Noticing*, there are only Light, Love, and Bliss.

---

[14] See above, n. 10. Also, see Philip Krill, *Le Point Vierge: Meditations on the Mystery of Presence.*

Our Relinquishment of mental interpretations enables others to blossom in our Presence. In the Space of Presence others *receive permission* to emerge from their egoic cocoons. Allowing ourselves and others simply to be, without criticism or comment, is more beneficial than all the altruism in the world.

The experience of Presence is always Fresh. It never grows stale. It is a Mystery that astounds us, even when we intentionally practice it. Presence is a Mystery of *existential immediacy*. It's like being gob-smacked by the Here-and-Now.

Peace can be found nowhere other than in Presence. If certain thoughts seem to bring Peace, it's only because they have momentarily brought our thinking to a stop. The Space *between our thoughts* is a main portal to Presence. The wider this Space, the deeper we enter into Presence.

Presence and thinking are not opposites. Thinking can never become Presence, but Presence can co-exist with and permeate our thoughts. When we are fully present, our thoughts and words emerge from Presence with a power they could not otherwise possess.

A person in Presence is bereft of ego but established in a transcendental identity. Ego, not identity, dissolves in Presence. Our transcendental identity in Presence is unknown to us, yet we are aware of ourselves as blessed recipients of Presence's self-communication. We are not nothing, but neither are we who we think we are.

Freedom means forsaking all to abide in Presence.

Freedom as choice disappears in Presence. In Presence, there is nothing more to say, nothing more to know, nothing more to desire. Presence silences deliberation.

Deliberation is for those still seeking Peace, but Peace can never be had as an outcome of deliberation. Peace arises only as a Gift of Presence. Deliberation is actually *despair* disguised as thoughtfulness.

Stop, look, and listen: This is good advice not only for those crossing railroad tracks but for everyone risking a train wreck by having a one-track mind.

Seeing is believing, yes, but it is also simply Beholding. When, in Presence, we simply *behold* the other, we connect with the other in a way that goes far beyond anything we might say in such an encounter. To paraphrase St. Francis of Assisi: be present always and use words only when necessary.

In Presence there is no forgiveness because there is nothing to forgive. There is nothing to forgive because Presence is benevolent Attentiveness without judgment or condemnation. We might say Presence is the Space of divine forgiveness trying to get us.

Everything is redeemed in the Space of Presence. Shame and guilt flee from the Now like the morning mist from the rising sun.

Looking back on our past mistakes is a bigger mistake than the mistakes of the past.

Looking for God in the future is a sure and certain way of missing God altogether, since there is never anything other than Now.

The epicenter of the present moment is not of this world. Living fully in the present, we are '*in* the world but not *of* it' (cf. Jn. 1:10; 17:6).

Regrets are the mother's milk of those who have not feasted on Presence. In Presence, our appetite for resentment disappears. Presence reveals remorse to be a waste of time.

The need for deliberate choice disappears in Presence. In Presence, deciding among alternatives becomes irrelevant. Wisdom comes naturally and without thinking in the Space of Presence.

Presence is trans-moral, a Mystery above and beyond the opposites of good and evil. Presence reveals as demonic the spirit of demonization that possess us when we eat from the *'the tree of the knowledge of good and evil'* (cf. Gen. 2:17). Presence shows evil to be the *division* of the world *into* good and evil. Presence delivers us from diabolic duality when we recognize its subtlety and ubiquity.

Approaching Presence is like trying to grasp the half-life of an isotope: it is never exhausted but infinitely recedes from our attempts to control it.

Regardless of our occupation, we are all called to discover and project Presence. A toolmaker who is fully present to his task exhibits more brilliance than a professor who can discuss Presence without knowing how to practice it.

Every endeavor is divinized when undertaken in Presence. Presence is not something done *in addition* to what we are doing. Presence is the *inner disposition of Watchfulness with which* we do what we are doing.

Are there persons whose sole calling in life is only to practice Presence? Whose only occupation is to be aware of Awareness? If so, they make the world better simply by walking around.

Whatever gives us Pause has the power to Awaken. When the synapses of our minds momentarily short-circuit, the Power of Presence fills the gap.

Presence is the vacuum tube in which the filaments of our minds shine most brightly and give their best kind of warmth.

The Serenity arising in Presence is not stoical in nature. It does not issue in indifference or cause our upper lips to stiffen. Rather, it is an *effervescent Joy* that is self-contained, even while it radiates its healing Power to others.

Presence is an experience of Relinquishment (*Gelassenheit*) without beginning or end. It is a bottomless 'Letting go.' The deeper our Letting go, the higher our Lifting up. Presence reveals death and resurrection as the selfsame Mystery.

There is no movement in Presence, save an ever-increasing Acuity of benevolent Attention. The eyes of persons in Presence are luminescent with a Light of Love without conditions. Persons in Presence are incapable of blaming or shaming.

Pure Awareness is our deepest nature, yet it takes our breath away each time we avert to it. Abiding in Awareness as our intrinsic nature is a participation in divine Bliss.

Presence renders everything within it as *pen-ultimate*. Presence *relativizes* every field of object awareness without itself being either field or object.

Assenting to ourselves as *fields of personal Presence,* we spiritualize the cosmos without trying. Presence manifests its Power more intensely whenever we embrace It intentionally.

Practicing Presence means intentionally opening to the Power of Be-ing. It is an exercise in *purposeful ignorance.* It is a discipline of self-forgetfulness such that we become all Receptivity. It is entering the Space of acute, No-mind Awareness.

Practicing Presence is the path to Freedom - freedom from ego, freedom from fear, freedom from mind-made suffering.

Entering Presence means exploring the infinite depths of *is-ing-ness.* Deeper and higher than thought, Presence takes us beyond this world without taking us out of it. We remain *in* the world but not *of* it.

The mind is a human survival machine. The problem is, egoic thoughts manufacture only suffering and illusions. Presence subverts mind-games from within. It dissolves the agonistic dichotomies of attack and rebuff, desire and defend. It moves us from *polarized misery* into a harmonious, heavenly way of living.

Our capacity for Presence reveals us as those who are 'there for' the other. '*We are here for you*' is something we can only say, and mean, when empowered by Presence. Being present means being in contact with the innermost being of the other, not just their persona. Integrity happens when our persona reflects an inner experience of Presence without interruption.

The best counselor is the person who can remain in Presence while the other is lost in the agony of a mind-stream or is drowning under a tsunami of emotion. The mental and emotional demons that haunt us can be driven out only by Presence.

Presence works like a Solvent on self-identification with either thought or emotion. Presence means discovering our true self as the *transcendent Witness* to our thoughts and feelings.

We are freed from our slavery to ego every time we discover our ability to stand outside ourselves as our own witnessing Presence.

Our ability to transcend our egoic selves reveals Presence as a Power both within and beyond us.

The power of Presence can always increase within us. The intensity of Presence is directly proportional to the *Relinquishment* of our critical thinking. The greater our inner self-emptying (*Kenosis, Gelassenheit*), the more fully we are permeated with the energy of Presence.

What religious people call 'holiness' means being *transfigured from within* by the experience of Presence. This experience arises the moment we shift from thinking to Awareness of our thinking. *Watching* ourselves think, we are *beyond* being hurt by our thoughts. Instead, a certain kind of divine Bliss begins, the Fulness (*Pleroma*) of which results in our divinization.

Personal selfhood is a participation in the Self - or the personal Selfhood of God - without being identical with it. Failure to distinguish, without separating, personal awareness from Awareness Itself (Presence) gives rise to every kind of pantheistic and theophanistic misunderstanding.

Consciousness *of* consciousness is ineluctably *personal*. Our sense of 'we' is not lost in our experience of Presence. On the contrary, it is enhanced and purified. Our sense of who 'we are' never dissolves like a drop of water in the ocean of Awareness. It is impossible to be Aware of Awareness without being *personally* aware of it. This gives the lie to *Advaita*.[15] On the other hand, the ineluctable 'us' experienced in Presence is also aware of itself *as beholden to*, and in the possession of, a Power greater than itself. It is aware of its own nothingness apart from this Power. Thus, personal identity in Presence is not egoic identity. Ego is the fruitless, unconscious attempt to secure a personal sense of self as if it did not derive from the Power of Presence that possesses it.

---

[15] See above, n. 5.

Presence reveals everything as essentially perfect. Nothing needs to be added to make us perfectly who we are. We are a Mystery unto ourselves, but a Mystery that is shown to be one with, yet distinct from, the Mystery of Presence that possesses us.

When we are caught up in Presence, we see who we truly are, yet also realize that our true selves are *hidden with God in Presence* (cf. Col. 3:3). Only God knows us as we truly are, since our personal identities derive from, and return to, the great I AM that is God (cf. Ex. 3:14; Rev. 2:17).

Guilt and shame are foreign to Presence. It's not simply that Presence banishes all guilt and shame - though it also does that - but it does not *comprehend* them. Nor do they comprehend Presence. Guilt and shame are natural derivatives of egoic interactions, projecting only darkness. Presence is Light that appears in the darkness and the darkness cannot comprehend It (cf. Jn. 1:5). Once the Light of Presence appears, the darkness is banished forever, and guilt and shame are revealed to be illusions of the ego.

Living in Presence is the antidote to living in the past or the future. In Presence, we experience a continuous rebirth such that we grow spiritually *younger* the longer we stay there. As the song, *Amazing Grace*, says, '*When we've been there ten thousand years, it will be as if we have just begun.*'

Thinking, disconnected from Presence, is insanity. The end of guilt - and of blaming and shaming - will never come so long as we believe there are good reasons for them. Reasoning apart from Presence generates oppression.

The world operates on the five R's: Rivalry, Resentment, Rage, Retaliation, Repeat. Or the five C's: Compare, Complain, Criticize, Condemn. In Presence, the five R's and the four C's melt away and are transformed into Kindness.

There is no explaining Presence. Presence is a *why-less Mystery* that makes possible our Awakening and transformation. Gratitude, not inquiry, is our proper response to the Self-communication of Presence.

# 10th

## Wicker Basket

Presence communicates directly, not conceptually. Innovation and creativity arise, not from intense thinking, but from a 'flash of inspiration' or an 'intuitive grasp' of a heretofore unimagined possibility. The Source of such 'flashes of insight' exceeds our cognitive powers. They come from Presence, the pre-eternal Condition for the possibility of existence. It is from Presence that all things, including our cognitive powers, derive. Creativity is always a matter of Presence communicating Itself more completely to those who know how to abide in Presence.

Presence is perceptiveness - a perspicacious Awareness of ourselves as mysteries of transcendent Consciousness. It also involves the recognition of others as equal, yet separate and unique, Mysteries of this same perspicacious Awareness. Such percipience issues automatically in sympathy, forgiveness, love and affection.

It is impossible to live in Presence without being suffused with its Uncreated Light. It is impossible not to love everything and everyone so long as we remain knowingly and intentionally in Presence.

The fact that it makes syntactic sense to say, 'remaining knowingly and intentionally in Presence,' is proof positive that a non-egoic, yet uniquely personal sense of self remains and is perfected in Presence.

In Presence, loving others strikes us as an *obligation*, not a matter of deliberation. It is a felt-sense of necessity, something we cannot not do. In Presence, the deliberative will is, as it were, anesthetized. The temptation not to love another in Presence is non-existent.

Presence is the Source of conscience, not the other way around. Conscience is not the ability to make the right decision, while choosing among many options, but the *inability to do anything other than love* in the most perfect way possible.

Presence puts us in touch with such an empathetic connection with others that any violation of this connection seems an evil of which we cannot conceive. This, in turn, reveals evil to be non-existent. Evil is not the opposite of love but its *absence*. Therefore, it is nothing at all. Presence, by contrast, is a Fulness (*Pleroma*) of Love which knows nothing of evil.

Absent a sense of Presence, we easily confuse conscience with super-ego. The ego, as Freud taught us, also has a super-ego - a superior voice of authority, reinforcing its fears, doubts, and insecurities, and proffering itself as the guarantor of our security. Presence renders the whole ego/super-ego structure irrelevant and unreal. To the extent that Presence is experienced, Love becomes connatural, and judgments between good and evil, right and wrong, disappear.

Presence, and those who live in Presence, inhabit a Space *beyond* good and evil. True Freedom means being *incapable* of doing anything that is not perfect in Love.

*Theosis* - deification or divinization - is the End for which every person is made. It is also the fruition of those who live knowingly in Presence. Divinization through Presence is the Gift and task of conscious humanity.

Presence absorbs evil like a good paper towel absorbs a spill. Presence makes evil disappear by assuming it into itself.

Though beyond religion, Presence admits of a trinitarian form. Though trans-ecclesiastical, Presence shows itself to be a triune Mystery. To wit: persons in Presence experience themselves in possession of a Power greater than themselves. One with us, yet greater than us (cf. Jn. 10:30; 14:28), the Power of Presence also communicates itself to others *through* us. Persons in Presence are also instruments of Presence.

Presence allows us to see the perfect purity of everything God has created. Presence is salvation, if salvation is defined as escape from guilt and shame, which occurs immediately once we behold creation from the place of Presence.

Presence reveals our inherent innocence, purity and guiltlessness. There is no condemnation in Presence (cf. Rom. 8:1). Since all things springs forth from the Wellspring of Presence, they can never be anything less than perfect. Any overlay of 'sin' may temporarily obscure, but leave entirely unharmed, our capacity for Presence.

Entering Presence is an ever-new experience. Our fears that Presence could ever leave us, or ever not deliver the ecstatic vision it brings, are banished as soon as felt-contact with Presence is regained.

In Presence we learn to trust what is necessary for us to know will be communicated when and how we require it. We also learn that the *sine quo non* for this communication is abandonment of our preconceived ideas.

In Presence, Presence gives the whole of Itself to us. In giving us Itself, Presence gives us all it knows and is.

Presence is never depleted, even though it gives *all* of Itself to those who abide in Presence. The self-communication of Presence is also the self-fulfillment of *Presence*. Presence replenishes *Itself* the more we experience Presence possessing and transfiguring us from within.

Presence has the power to dissolve empires. In the face of pure evil, Presence proves Itself capable of disarming it. Often this victory involves the death of the person faced with a political or personal monster; but, every evil is overcome, not through opposition with egoic force, but with Presence manifesting itself though persons practicing Presence, especially amidst persecution.

Every interaction among persons who know nothing of Presence is an event of persecution. Political and inter-personal relationships are disguised as the *status quo*. Presence reveals every *status quo* to be an illusion of the collective ego. Presence makes possible a community of Peace inhabited by those who knowingly practice Presence.

Helping professionals who do anything other than model of Presence to those they serve do them a disservice. Without Presence, professional counseling is a form of implicit condescension, bereft of the Kindness only Presence can deliver.

The Wellspring of Presence never runs dry. We can go to it a million times a day and never be disappointed. It's as if Presence is waiting for us, completing Itself by giving Itself to us.

Presence relativizes our human bonds of love, while simultaneously strengthening them. In Presence we discover a sense of fulfillment no human relationship can give, while at the same time we are enabled to love everyone with purer, stronger Love.

Presence dispels relationship fatigue and makes intimacy possible, even with total strangers. Jealousy and concupiscence are neutralized when we enter Presence.

The attempt to experience the present moment is to already have entered Presence. Presence arises the moment we stop thinking and shift to thoughtless Awareness.

Presence enters our world at the indefinable point of the Pause. Like a teacher capturing the Attention of her students by lifting an object in the air and saying, 'Look here!', in this momentary shift in Attention, the Peace of Presence arises.

One mili-second of Pause - of Presence - redeems a lifetime of mental and emotional pressure.

Whatever we call it - Nirvana, Enlightenment, Salvation - is simply abiding in Presence as often as possible.

When we are present to our thoughts, we are shown to be beyond our thoughts. This revelation of self-transcendence is an intuitive by-product of practicing Presence.

We can be present to ourselves, showing that self-transcendence is our inherent nature, and that it is Infinite. There is no end to the Depths to which we can stand back from ourselves and observe ourselves. Somehow we are an infinite microcosm of a Macrocosm of infinite Presence.

No one can speak authentically of Presence without returning again and again to the primordial *experience* of Presence. Sometimes it takes a lifetime (or more) before it dawns on us that thinking about and practicing Presence are worlds apart. This 'dawning upon' is called *satori* or salvation.

Presence cannot be truly spoken or written about without Presence itself exercising an editorial function. Only certain words, expressed in certain ways, possess the power to reveal Presence. It is Presence Itself that inspires these words and does the Awakening.

If we place our *grief* in Presence, it relativizes our pain, making our grief redemptive and keeping us from questioning God. If we place our *joy* in Presence, it relativizes our exuberance, preventing us from forgetting God in its Afterglow.

Presence functions like a car's automatic emergency braking system: it keeps us from plowing into anyone ahead of us, and from backing into anyone behind us. It creates a cone of safety in which we can maintain our bearings even when traveling at breakneck speed on the highway of life.

Presence means cultivating inner Spaciousness. It is a matter of surrounding our thoughts and emotions with the bubble wrap of Acceptance and non-judgment.

Presence is a *Plenitude (Pleroma)* that never fails to deliver divine Bliss without being depleted. For those learning the difference between thinking and being present, the Peace that comes from Presence seems too good to be true. Sometimes fear creeps in, saying Presence cannot always make good on its promise. These fears too, once placed in Presence, dissipate. One learns to access Presence, not as an emotional placebo, but as a sacred Invitation never to be withdrawn.

Bliss and gratitude are the invariant by-products of discovering Presence. They never grow old, only more profound.

Presence has *us*, not us It. In Presence, we Awaken to a pre-existent Power of Serenity that all the evil in the world cannot disturb. It is truly the *'Peace that passes all understanding'* (cf. Phil. 4:7).

Hopes and aspirations for world Peace are made possible by the Fulness of the Peace already present in Presence. We need travel no further than our own inner capacity for letting-go (*Gelassenheit*) to enter the only Utopia we will ever find.

Presence is discovered in every act of Releasement. The Germans call it *Gelassenheit*: Relinquishment, Surrender, Detachment. We can also call it *Letting-go-ness*. In every act of self-emptying (*Kenosis*), self-actualization takes place.

We find our lives when we are self-*dis*-possessed. Presence is the perfect state of *self-dis-possession*, i.e., attentive Awareness devoid of agenda.

If it's true that life is not worth living unless, and until, we find something worth dying for, then it is especially true that intentional *'dying to self'* is the only real path to Life. Presence is the practice of *dying before we die.*

*Philip Krill*

Presence and prayer exhibit the same posture: Openness to the Infinite. Prayer and Presence become a single action when prayer divests itself of words and ideas.

Presence is both a practice and a posture. Presence requires practice until it becomes our natural *modus operandi*. When that happens we become contemplatives in action, without ceasing to pray contemplatively.

# 11th

# Wicker Basket

Our initial experience of Presence can obliterate ego completely, though for most of us Presence is glimpsed in brief flashes at first, giving us time to process its Power, and revealing the ego's resistance to this invasion of its territory.

Everyone experiences Presence in the *gaps* between thinking and doing, but few *recognize* it as such. Fewer still recognize these flashes of Presence as the Light of God dispelling the darkness in their lives. Only a very select few sell all that they have, egoically speaking, to acquire this Pearl of Great Price (cf. Mt. 13:44-46).

Presence is spacious Openness, Openness to what is Other. As such, Presence reveals a symbiosis with *all* that is other from us. Symbiosis, however, is not identity. Presence suggests that our Openness is somehow *completed* by the other, yet also makes clear that the experience of Presence is *fulfilling in itself*. Presence is what makes our appreciation of otherness possible, while the Bliss of Presence arises even in the absence of any 'other.'

Presence is a *'prepositional'* Mystery. Presence is always 'Presence *for*' and 'Presence *to*,' even when no objects inhabit its Space. Presence is spacious Availability for all, even when no others are present.

Presence is like the Emptiness of a room that remains unaffected by the objects placed within it. Presence is like a movie screen that makes possible, yet stays untouched, by the images that appear upon it. *That which makes possible* object consciousness is itself not an object. Presence is the most real thing there is, but it cannot be objectified.

In Presence, distinctions are recognized and differences acknowledged, but notions of division or dichotomous thinking disappear.

In Presence, any sense of alienation is instantly overcome. Comparisons do not exist, complaining doesn't occur, criticism cease, and condemnation never takes place. What religious persons call 'sin' is inconceivable in Presence.

We cannot be awash in Presence and still feel the need to cleanse themselves of guilt and shame. 'Forgiveness' is too anodyne a term to describe the trans-ethical Alleviation of remorse afforded by Presence.

Presence reveals 'sin' to be not transgressions against a heteronomous, authoritative figure or code, but a web of *positionalities* - thoughts, opinions, ideations - held together by vanity and fear. In other words, 'sin' is *ego* in all its deceptive, accusatory, and divisive forms. All of these Presence undoes with a single Touch of its infinite Power.

Knowingly entering Presence for the first time feels like being born anew (cf. Jn. 3:3-7). It represents a reversal of Esau selling his birthright for a pottage of lentils (cf. Gen. 25:33). In Presence we exchange a lifetime of guilt for an eternity of innocence.

Presence is a repudiation of labeling. Pigeonholes are foreign to Presence. Presence is the Spaciousness that allows all things to be just as they are. The Being and becoming of things which appear in Presence are given all the room they need to both reveal and conceal themselves. For every being (object) is a non-exhaustive revelation of Being ('God,' the uncreated Source of beings), at once disclosing and masking from Whence it comes.

Presence is the paradox of perfect Receptivity and non-reactivity. In Presence, judgment is held in abeyance, while empathic Attentiveness is fully operative. Empty of all expectations, Presence is filled with Acceptance and Understanding. A sense of divine Bliss is concomitant with every experience of Presence.

When we are in Presence, everything outside of Presence seems an illusion. If entering Presence is like awakening from a nightmare, living outside of Presence is spiritual sleep walking.

What passes for knowledge in the egoic world is an accumulation of labels. Words and ideas are not the things they refer to. Descriptions give us a false sense of security, a false sense of knowledge, a false sense of power. Presence, by contrast, is a luminous Cloud of Unknowing. It allows objects to manifest their inherent Mystery without cognitive commentary. Presence permits the depth of Being to appear, while ego obscures it.

In Presence, there is no melodrama. Presence is the *Power of the Now* in which problems from the past or fears about future are replaced by the Bliss of the present moment. It is impossible to have any problems in the sheer Actuality of the Now.

A person who cultivates Presence is the best possible friend for those still mired in the story-driven drama of egoic existence, not because of what they say but because of who they are. Presence is contagious. Presence works by osmosis. Presence communicates itself, not with words, but with Power. The silent, accepting Spaciousness emanating from Presence has a healing effect upon everyone and everything in its orbit. Even plants and animals experience the curative power of Presence. The person in Presence restores others to wholeness just by walking around.

Presence fills us with humility and power. Like a filament in a lightbulb, we are lit up from within by a Power greater than ourselves. We are aware we are one with, yet distinct from, this Power greater than ourselves. We shine brightly with a Light that originates beyond ourselves.

Those who practice Presence are teachers of Innocence. Without saying a word, they reveal an inherent 'virginal spirit' that they and all persons possess.

To make the Shift from pondering to Presence is to re-acquire a childlike Wonder in which pre-judgments are suspended, guilt is banished, shame and accusation are unknown, and supernatural Bliss overflows naturally.

There is a certain blessedness in being able to say, 'I don't know.' Admission of ignorance is disarming when it flows from Presence. For Presence is a state of perpetual Unknowing that gives us a Peace the world cannot give (cf. Jn. 14:27). It imparts a Wisdom that transcends intellectual reduction. Admission of ignorance opens a Space where persons meet each other in Wisdom and Peace.

Presence is a Space of divine Alchemy. In Presence, the lead of our thoughts become the gold of divine Intuition. Wisdom is given us intuitively in Presence that escapes rational analysis.

Presence is like a just-in-time delivery service. In Presence, we are given what we need when we need it - no sooner, no later. No haste, no waste. Presence is leaner and cleaner than any human production system.

Presence is the Space of perfect Openness, devoid of expectations but saturated with Receptivity. The Emptiness of Presence is the Fulness of Love.

Objects in the world change and morph into different configurations with kaleidoscopic beauty and bewilderment. Trying to stop or compartmentalize this process results in insanity. Presence is untouched by the chaos of change, making it possible for us to perceive transcendent Beauty with every turn of the kaleidoscope.

It is impossible to be upset in Presence. Bliss is its constant accompaniment. This occurs because Presence takes us beyond thinking into an Ocean of unrestricted Awareness where our thoughts cannot tread water for long before drowning in a Sea of Light and Joy.

Presence permeates our very somatic structure. Our chakras sing with the silent Music of Presence. Our extremities resonate with the Power of Presence. Our eyes - the windows of our souls - shine luminescent with the Light of Presence.

Our bodies are sacramental instruments of Presence. Inhabiting our bodies with Attentiveness takes us away from thinking into Presence. Experiencing Presence begins and ends with being present to - and in - our bodies.

Presence is greater than that which is known as Ki (or Chi). Ki is, as it were, a bridge of energy between Presence and the world of forms.

Boredom is banished when we live in Presence. Every moment is exhilarating, filled with an intuitive sense of the Fulness (*Pleroma*) of Being. Time disappears when we live in Presence, whereas boredom fills the time when our connection with Presence is broken.

The original sin is to confuse thinking with Presence. It is to *'eat from the tree of the knowledge of good and evil'* (cf. Gen. 2:17). In so doing, we poison ourselves with mental judgments. Presence is our antidote to this deadly poison. Only thoughts arising unbidden in the Space of Presence are worth listening to.

Those who Awaken know what it is to sleep, but those who are still asleep do not know what it is to be Awake.

Presence is existential contact with Reality. Conceptualization is experiencing reality at a remove. Presence is Truth, systematic ideation an illusion.

In Presence, there is no argumentation. With conceptual thinking, there is *nothing but* argumentation. These arguments need not be acrimonious but they are inevitable.

Presence challenges every system of reason to examine its preconditions, while Presence knows itself to be the silent Source of such cognition. Every form of reasoning is dependent upon a prior set of irreducible and unprovable assumptions. Presence, aware of this fact, waits upon reason to discover Presence as its ultimate precondition.

Recognizing the limits of pure reason is a revelation of reason's subsistence in Presence. Only in Presence can one reason rightly. Pure reason can never attain to Presence.

Persons lost in a labyrinth of thought can easily dismiss Presence as pie-in-the-sky, New Age mumbo jumbo, much like some atheists dismiss belief in 'God' as a form of wish-fulfillment (Freud) or as an opiate of ignorant people (Marx). Such discounting of Presence makes sense to persons enmeshed in the predicaments caused by their critical thinking. For those who step back from the chaos created by such thinking, the inherent limitations of the mind are revealed, and the Peace afforded by Presence comes to light. It is when we become conscious of our own thinking processes that we are no longer enslaved by them.

Our experience of Presence is a participation in an unspeakable Effulgence of Being (*Sat*), Consciousness (*Chit*) and Bliss (*Ananda*). What we call 'God' is the ineffable coincidence of Being, Consciousness and Bliss in which our experience of Presence (*Saccidananda*) subsists.

Presence is an experience of being arrested by the existence and implicate order of all that is. Presence is an act of perpetually astonished Beholding. Presence beholds the fact that existence is, at every moment, unnecessary in itself, unable to account for its own being, yet miraculously sustained by a Power found nowhere in the order of existing things. Presence is the Awareness that no object, nor the entire universe of objects, is the Source of its own existence. Presence is the Space of continuous Astonishment at Being.

When we are astonished by something, we are, momentarily, 'out of our minds.' That is, our thinking is interrupted by something we find so arresting that our mental movements are put on Pause and we experience a moment of Presence. Living a contemplative life means expanding this capacity for Presence, extending our ability to be amazed and astonished at the simple fact of Being. Everything is beautiful when beheld in Presence.

In Presence, we are aware of ourselves as the Beholder, beholding our Beholding. Yet, we can never fully 'see' ourselves as this Beholder. The one who 'Beholds our Beholding' eludes our grasp. 'We' are the condition for the possibility of our own Beholding. This pre-conceptual 'we' is as real as it is indefinable. We can only allude to it, though we are always implicitly aware of it.

Whatever beliefs we espouse sound like hollow pontifications if not rooted in Presence. What we believe is believable only if *we* are believable in proclaiming them. But if that is the case - and Presence is the proof of authenticity - why proclaim such beliefs at all? Wouldn't the Truth of such beliefs come from and return to Presence?

Awakening to Presence, we find ourselves freed from resentment and expectations. We have entered a Space of *Gelassenheit* - 'Letting-go-ness' or 'Allowing-ness.'[16] In this Space of Releasement, conceptual identity - ego - is non-existent. The Beauty of the Now is self-evident. There, silence speaks and inward stillness reigns. In Presence we realize there is no such thing as nothingness. We experience Absence as another form of Presence, and 'difference' or 'otherness' as an ecstatic expression of a an ever-greater Fulness (*Pleroma*).

---

[16] See Philip Krill, *Gelassenheit: Day-by-Day with Meister Eckhart.*

Presence sanctifies the Space that thought defines as 'separation.' Presence reveals divisions, dichotomies, and dialectics as forms of deception.

Presence is a Power greater than those who experience it. It's as if Presence needs persons to reveal its transcendent Power. We participate in Presence, but Presence itself is a Mystery which is unparticipatible. Persons *allow* the Power of Presence to manifest Itself, but our capacity for Presence is made possible by the Power of Presence itself.

Presence is a *Power*, not an object. Yet, even as a *'Power,'* Presence is not a thing. Describing Presence as a *noun* is misleading, even if our language affords us no other option. Like the breeze fluttering the leaves of a tree, the arising of Presence is always an *event*, never simply an action. It is a momentary entrée into pure Actuality, an instantaneous Intuition of ultimate Being.

Practicing Presence never grows old, but must be continually refreshed. It can never be programmed, only continually pursued; never captured, but constantly desired. Experiencing Presence takes constant effort, but always comes to us as a Gift.

How does a person cultivate Presence? By being the *Space* for anything that arises in the present moment. *Kenosis, Gelassenheit,* self-Emptying: this is the disposition that makes our experience of Presence possible.

Identification with our thoughts is the biggest obstacle to getting into contact with and remaining in Presence. Egoic thinking blocks our Openness to the Now.

For those who believe in God, they might try saying, 'God is Now-ing us.' Those who do not believe in God might simply say, 'The Now is Now-ing us,' Regardless of our beliefs, it takes no time at all to live as 'we are.' It takes no time at all to live in the Now.

Reactivity, defensiveness, is always a function of ego. It comes from resisting the form of the present moment, not realizing that 'this too will pass.' Such behavior is impossible in Presence. Presence is the Power of Allowing-ness. When we *allow* Being to be as it is, not as we would want it, our problems disappear. If situational challenges remain, they are seen more clearly in Presence, and the Wisdom to know how to handle them is given us.

Difficult people and situations are prime opportunities to deepen our practice of Presence. They remind us to default to Presence instead of losing ourselves in the egoic drama that consumes so many persons' lives.

Fear, doubt, and insecurity contain the seeds of their own subversion. When they become catalysts for our return to Presence, they disappear. Evil is the illusion of those who have not yet found their way into Presence.

Humor is Presence putting a smile on our face. It elevates our vision beyond the deadly dialectics of thinking. Angels can fly because they take themselves lightly.

Pain is not suffering. Suffering occurs when the pain of life is not accepted for what it is. When pain is received knowingly in Presence, it doesn't become less painful, but it is 'suffered,' i.e., allowed to be. Redemptive suffering is pain redeemed by Presence.

Possessions, accolades, fame, money, status - none of these can give us what Presence can give. Lots of people flying in private jets are miserable. There is no aircraft in the world that can transport us into the heavenly Space of Presence.

The journey to the stars - or anywhere on earth - is always *inward*, never outward. The Vision that impels great explorers comes from within, not from without. We will never find Utopia anywhere other than in the place of Presence. Trying to change external circumstances is always a bit like re-arranging the deck chairs on the Titanic. Presence is the lifeboat that can save us from the shipwreck of misplaced attention.

# 12th

# Wicker Basket

Once we despair of the ability of external states of affairs to make us happy, we experience a surprisingly fresh capacity to appreciate them. It's only when we don't *need* to have someone or something to make us happy that we regain our capacity to be happy. Presence is the Space of 'not needing' (egoic dependence) yet also of 'happy to have' (joyful gratitude).

Griping about life is replaced by Gratitude in the place of Presence.

Without Presence, expectations of others quickly suffocate relationships. Expectations become demands, demands cause suffering, suffering leads to scapegoating, and scapegoating results in resentment, rage, and the felt need to retaliate. Presence puts *breathing room* into relationships. It gives others Space to be themselves, without expectations. The great paradox is this: the less pressure, the greater the performance; the fewer the expectations, the greater the satisfaction.

Intimacy is a function of Letting go, not holding on. Letting go (*Gelassenheit*) is our entrance into Presence. Love is a function more of freedom than of forgiveness. For persons relating in Presence, there is nothing to forgive.

In Presence, thoughts come and go like clouds in the sky. The sky, however, is empty Space. Presence is that heavenly, interior Emptiness where thoughts are allowed to pass through unimpeded. We may well notice them, but we find our Noticing more inspiring than the thoughts we notice. The last thing we want to do is *think about* how we can get rid of our thoughts.

Presence is the Mystery of interior Poverty from which Wisdom, the only true wealth, emerges. It is in the Awareness of our nothingness that everything we need is given. Our Awareness that all is Gift is the greatest Gift we can receive.

Persons living in Presence are continually surprised and amazed at the prescience of the inspirations that come to them. If they are believers, they are wont to say, 'God's timing is always perfect.' If they prefer a more pedestrian form of expression, they might say, 'Presence is the world's best just-in-time delivery system.' In Presence what we need to know, and what we need to do (or not do), is given precisely when it is needed, not a moment sooner or later. And all of this is simply the Mystery of Now demonstrating its Power.

Persons operating from Presence need neither talking points nor scripts to inform what they say or believe. The Power of the Now resists the written word. Or better, only words written under the influence of Presence have real Power. There is a world of difference between explaining and *proclaiming*, between describing and *declaring*. For a person filled with Presence, even their explaining and describing appear to be infused with a kind of prophetic Power.

Presence is an indictment of every *status quo*. Presence is a scandal - an offensive stumbling block - for those who identify with the *status quo*. And this, regardless of political or religious persuasion. For the *status quo* is nothing other than a structured egoic illusion, a collective conceptual perspective. Presence stands outside consensus. Presence is impervious to politics or religion. Presence, in fact, is what every system is searching for, but can never find, in its efforts at self-justification and self-preservation.

Paragons of Presence - Buddha, Socrates, Jesus - often find themselves martyred by the *status quo*. 'Martyr' means 'witness.' Such martyrs witness to a Power that transcends death. Because they live in Presence, they experience only compassion for their persecutors.

Persons living in Presence know when enough is enough. They know when to speak and when to keep quiet. They know when to write, and when to stop writing. They have an impeccable sense of timing because they operate outside time.

Those who write, speak or act from Presence do not worry about the Wellspring of their inspiration running dry. They recognize every such anxiety as a deception of the ego.

A person operating in Presence resembles a tightrope walker working without a net, or an Olympic athlete performing on the balance beam. They make look easy what, for most people, proves impossible. This is because they are not aware of the consequences of their actions but are entirely focused, without thought, on what's right in front of them. One step at a time, they prove their doubters wrong.

Presence is a place of pure Relaxation. It is without tension. It is the Space of expectant Listening. Expectant, because out of Presence emerges unanticipated discernment and direction. Listening, because in Presence nothing can be heard until the voice in our heads is silenced.

Resistance to Presence seems almost endemic to being human. Ego has a thousand masks. Every moment is a new Invitation, a new Opportunity, a new challenge to acknowledge the persistence of ego and, in accepting it, to practice Presence.

Presence means putting the Space of Acceptance around every manifestation of ego. Anxiety is a reminder to bring more Presence into any situation.

There is no limit to the Depths of Letting go connected to the practice of Presence. We can always become more Receptive, more Open, more benignly Alert. A fathomless, poised Docility characterizes those who know how to be Present. They have soft, keen eyes, devoid of judgment but filled with compassionate Understanding.

Persons who practice Presence are generally happy wherever they may be. This is because their Joy is rooted, not in external situations, but in an interior reservoir of unconditioned Being. They are aware of their own miraculous 'we-are-ness,' and they behold that same 'Gratuity of Being' in every person and circumstance they encounter. Their Consciousness (*Chit*) of Being (*Sat*) is Bliss (*Ananda*).

One of the paradoxes of Presence is this: when, in Presence, we are able to 'stand back' from any situation and simply 'allow it to be,' we are given, in that Space of 'standing back from' or 'Allowing' (Presence), the Wisdom to know how to be helpful. The less egoically involved we are, the more lovingly helpful we can be.

Presence makes possible the union of Love and Freedom, Intimacy and Otherness. Presence is the Power that acknowledges *differences* but prevents *divisions*; that recognizes *diversity* but maintains *unity*; that affirms *alterity* while preventing *alienation*. Only in Presence can we do relationships right.

A person in Presence is comfortable when nothing is happening. Absence, for them, is another invitation to practice Presence. They never need to 'kill time,' since, for them, every moment is filled with a manifestation of Being.

The drama of everything re-framed in Presence is diminished. Presence relativizes the tragic events placed within it. Presence is like the Ocean: no matter how large or threatening the object placed within it, the gentleness of the water eventually dissolves the threat.

Egoic persons are like obstreperous children, while Presence is like a wise and knowing mother. The children may come kicking and screaming, but held close to her heart, they wear themselves out and fall asleep. The Embrace of Presence quiets our crying and screaming.

The admonition to 'pray without ceasing' means to practice Presence continuously; to bring Presence into every situation, every encounter.

Presence manifested in one person can awaken Presence in another. What would it take for a critical mass of humanity to awaken to Presence? Persons in Presence don't ask such questions. Better to light a single candle (Presence) than to curse the darkness.

Persons in Presence judge no one. They keep their eyes on their own plates. They stay in their own lanes. Yet, their hearts are filled with compassion for their fellow diners, their fellow travelers.

Bliss is fairly continuous for those who dwell in Presence. They *experience* the fact that they are not the Source of their own being. The Mystery of their own 'is-ing-ness' constantly astounds them and fills them with Joy. They blissfully realize they are sustained in being by a Power greater than themselves, which itself is the Fulness (*Pleroma*) of Being (*Sat*), Consciousness (*Chit*) and Bliss (*Ananda*).

Persons living in Presence have food the egoic world knows not of. They don't have to go out for dinner to enjoy a feast. They feast continuously on the bread of life - the hidden manna of their inner connection with the Power of Presence. They have only to shift from thinking to Awareness to be fully nourished.

Persons who practice 'being present' are never bored. Everything is interesting to them, including 'doing nothing.' They 'do nothing' really well. They don't mind waiting in line, being delayed, or cancelling something altogether. Open to the power and opportunities of the present moment, they have discovered that good things come to those who wait.

'Only fools rush in.' 'What a difference a day makes.' What do such clichés tell us? Just this: without Presence many things bring suffering, but with Presence, all things are possible.

The Mystery of the present moment is mentally ungraspable. Pure Actuality cannot be captured in a concept. It has to be experienced. It is an 'Intuition of Being,' a flash of Awakening (Enlightenment). It is the miracle of Presence.

Those who write or speak of Presence can make no end of it. This is because the experience of Presence is always fresh, always immediate, truly inexhaustible. One thinks of the tune, *How Can We Keep from Singing?*

Those who experience Presence always seem to get younger, never older. This is because, in Presence, they have transcended time. Neither do they fear death, for they have died to the thoughts that instill the fear of death.

In Presence, all things are reconciled, both in heaven and on earth. Presence is an alienation-free, mystical Space. Animosity and antagonism are unknown to persons abiding in Presence. All things appear beautiful to them, because they discern a transcendent Source of Goodness, Beauty, Truth, and Love from which all things come and to which all things return. Presence is the Mystery in which all things live and move and have their being (cf. Acts 17:28).

Presence is the Space in which differences are not only allowed to appear, but allowed to show themselves in their unique, incomparable glory. Presence differentiates, and perfect Presence differentiates perfectly.

Presence is God's greenhouse where all things are allowed to grow to their full potential.

Presence is the only place where persons can truly be themselves.

Anything beheld in Presence blooms. As an ancient proverb has it: 'I said to the almond tree, 'Speak to me of God,' and it blossomed.'

Presence is not the opposite of anything. It is beyond good and evil, beyond the difference between finite and infinite. It is the Light in which we see light, and the Light in which we experience the infinite Power of Letting Be.

Presence is the bond of communion between persons. It is not our thoughts, words, or actions that bind us to, or alienate us from, others. It is the Presence with which we enact them.

Presence is the healing balm of God.

If we are persons of Presence, we will never have to give lectures to anyone about anything. If we are not persons of Presence, even if we do, no one will believe us.

In Presence, we can look upon an entire lifetime of wasted time and find it immediately redeemed, such is the saving Power of Presence.

Everything is aglow with the glory of God in the Mystery of Presence.

Printed in the United States
by Baker & Taylor Publisher Services